CONTAINER GARDENS

CONTAINER GARDENS

OVER 200 FRESH IDEAS FOR INDOOR AND OUTDOOR PLANTINGS

By the Editors of **Southern Living**

Oxmoor
House®

©2017 Time Inc. Books

Published by Oxmoor House, an imprint
of Time Inc. Books
225 Liberty Street, New York, NY 10281

Southern Living is a registered trademark
of Time Inc. Lifestyle Group.

Senior Editor: Rachel Quinlivan West
Project Editor: Melissa Brown
Designer: Allison Chi
Garden Expert and Writer:
    Catherine Hall Kirpalani
Photographers: Ralph Lee Anderson,
    Van Chaplin, Erica George Dines,
    Roger Foley, Ryann Ford, Laurey W. Glenn,
    David Hillegas, Becky Luigart-Stayner,
    Wynn Meyers, Alison Miksch,
    Helen Norman, Lauren Rubenstein
Prop Stylists: Jan Gautro,
    Heather Chadduck Hillegas,
    Buffy Hargett Miller, Elly Poston
Prop Assistant: Gil Weingarten
Prop Coordinator: Audrey Davis
Assistant Production Director:
    Sue Chodakiewicz
Senior Production Manager: Greg A. Amason
Copy Editors: Rebecca Brennan,
    Polly Linthicum
Proofreader: Adrienne Davis
Indexer: Mary Ann Laurens
Fellows: Helena Joseph,
    Hailey Middlebrook,
    Kyle Grace Mills

On the Cover:
Photograph by Hector Manuel Sanchez
Prop styling by Buffy Hargett Miller

ISBN-13: 978-0-8487-4581-3
Library of Congress Control Number:
2016958805

First Edition 2017

Printed in the United States of America

10 9 8 7 6 5 4 3 2 1

We welcome your comments and suggestions
about Time Inc. Books.
Please write to us at:
Time Inc. Books
Attention: Book Editors
P.O. Box 62310
Tampa, Florida 33662-2310

Time Inc. Books products may be purchased
for business or promotional use. For
information on bulk purchases, please
contact Christi Crowley in the Special Sales
Department at (845) 895-9858.

Contents

GREATER IMPACT

Containers can offer a continuation of your planting theme in the garden, and coordinating those colors creates more impact in any space. Here, the white of the hydrangeas in the garden is repeated in the white petunias in the pots.

THE BASICS OF
Container
Gardening

AN INVITING ENTRANCE

Combining evergreens and annuals creates an interesting, welcoming entry year-round. With an open entry, like the one seen here, opt for tall evergreens like cypress. You can then vary the look seasonally by using bright annuals in the spring and summer, then changing them out for fall and winter plants.

GETTING
Started

It really doesn't matter where you live, how large your home,
or what your experience level may be, anyone can be a successful
container gardener. Few sights are more welcoming than lovingly tended
plants flourishing in beautiful containers. It's the best way to give
plants everything they need to grow and look their best.

Often the soil around your home isn't ideal for long-term gardening success because it's usually made up of a thin layer of topsoil spread over the compacted subsoil after construction. It's enough for a lawn to grow in the short run, but it's not ideal for the long haul. Plants won't be able to thrive without loosening and enriching the soil, which can be expensive in terms of both time and materials.

When you garden in a container, your commitment is more limited and manageable. Simply fill a generously sized pot with a quality potting mix and select plants that will enjoy the sun or shade where you plan to place the pot. With adequate light and a little care, plants will thrive. Gardening in containers gives you control—or as much control as you will experience when working with Mother Nature.

WHY GARDEN IN CONTAINERS?

Container gardening allows you to have living plants almost anywhere you want: atop paving, on a wall, hanging from a beam, or wherever fresh foliage and flowers are desired. You can create compositions and groupings that aren't possible in garden beds by moving the pots a few inches or elevating a couple to the perfect height. Best of all, they aren't expensive to maintain or time-consuming to keep looking fresh.

Gardening in pots can and should be simple as well as rewarding. While containers do need attention, the maintenance is relatively minimal—a few minutes of watering and removing dead flowers or yellowed leaves can keep them healthy. Whether you want your garden to have more color, your landscape more structure, or your table or windowsill more homegrown vegetables and herbs, container gardening can be the answer.

DESIGNING YOUR CONTAINERS

The key to creating beautiful containers is choosing appropriate pots, filling them with the right potting mix, and adding plants you like and that will thrive together. It's important to take into account the color, texture, and shape of the plants; the location of the pots; and to remember that all the plants growing in the same pot should be compatible. They must prosper in the same sun exposure and require a similar level of moisture so they can coexist happily for the season to come.

THE
Anatomy
OF A POT

If you're not sure what size container you need, choose the largest one that your porch, deck, or garden can accommodate and be in scale. Having a pot that is too small is like having a holiday wreath that isn't large enough for your door. It is doomed to be unremarkable. However, a pot that is a little bit large is forgivable, especially if the plantings are lovely. While styles and materials vary widely, there are some basic considerations:

SHAPE

The shape of the pots you need will be influenced by where they will be placed, the design of the home or outdoor space, and your personal preference. All shapes will support plant growth, but not all shapes make the removal of plants easy. It's more difficult to remove established plants and their roots from pots with rims that are narrower than the "belly." You may need to use a knife to cut the roots into pieces in order to slip the plant out of the narrow neck. Plan ahead and your seasonal transition will be easier.

PROPORTION

Pots can be tall and slender, squat and broad, or somewhere in between. Vertical containers lend themselves to narrow spaces, as well as places where you want emphasis, such as the corner of the pool or porch. They are inherently contemporary and have the advantage of raising your plants higher to be enjoyed up close.

Low bowls are ideal for shallow-rooted plants such as succulents, as well as for groupings where the other pots are taller. Broad and easily enjoyed, bowls are viewed from above like a stage viewed

from a balcony seat—and they are fun to plant.

Rectangular pots are boundary setters and passageway pots. They are usually planted with one kind of plant, or if mixed, the planting is often symmetrical.

The traditional form of terra-cotta pots, found everywhere from grandmother's garage to the modern garden center, remains round, tapering toward a base that is narrower than the rim. The height and width are basically equal. In smaller sizes the rim is a collar that makes the pot easy to grip with a thumb inside and index finger under the collar. It's no wonder it remains a classic.

WALLS

The thickness of the pot's walls can vary from a few millimeters of plastic resin to several inches of concrete or cast stone. A thick wall can be durable in hot and cold weather and less likely to be damaged in windy areas, but it definitely cuts down on the volume of potting mix that can be used. Less room for roots means less room for you to plant. Less potting mix means you will need to water and fertilize more often.

GET THE LOOK

Bright pink and yellow zinnias are the stars of these containers. Fill in with cooler "filler" flowers, such as purple verbena and blue calibrachoa to create contrast with texture and color. When the containers are placed side by side, all the colors intensify.

DRAINAGE MATTERS

Many gardeners faithfully use gravel (or shipping peanuts, pinecones, crushed aluminum cans, etc.) in the bottom of their pots to facilitate drainage. But if there's an adequate way for excess water to exit the pot, this step isn't necessary, and if there's no drainage, this actually won't help. The gravel will fill with water, and the moisture will wick upwards, keeping the potting mix too wet. Also, if you're using a pot that has limited room for roots, putting this layer of debris in the bottom leaves less room for the potting mix in which your plants can thrive.

In the rare case where the pot is much larger than the plants will need, you can partially fill the base with this type of filler and cover it with landscape fabric to prevent the potting mix from washing into it. However, a drainage hole is still needed. If the pot is tall, use a heavy filler like granite gravel to prevent the pot from tipping over.

RIMS ▲

The top edge that is so frequently concealed by overhanging and trailing plants can have a surprising impact on the appearance of a container planting. A thick, swollen rim is easy to grip and not so easy to break. No matter what type of container you're using, a pot that appears well made and sturdy gives a better impression. Pots that are made of thin material look best when the rim is turned inward, creating the illusion of a thick rim.

THE FOOT ▶

This ridge around the outer edge at the bottom of the pot lifts it slightly from the surface below. Not all pots have a foot.

Mesh screen

Mesh screen and pebbles

Rocks

DRAINAGE ▲

With the exception of water garden pots, all planted pots, even big ones, must have a hole for excess water to drain away from the potting soil. If not, the roots will drown. To prevent potting mix from washing out of the bottom of the pot, use a coffee filter; large mesh screen, such as a piece of hardware cloth; pebbles; rocks; or even a broken piece of terra-cotta pottery. Place a curved piece of terra-cotta over the drainage hole so that the curve is up, creating a small canopy over the hole.

Having a foot (see opposite page) helps a pot drain. Otherwise, containers with drainage holes on the bottom can be easily sealed as they rest directly on a flat surface. With these pots, use pot feet, little clay or concrete props that lift the container off the ground. They also allow the surface below the pot to dry, preventing rot on wooden porches and decks. Use three for a round pot and four for a square or rectangular pot for ample and even support. If you don't have pot feet, use bricks or flat stones of similar thickness to raise the pot.

You'll notice some pots have a concave bottom that keeps the drainage hole an inch or so off the surface below and prevents blockage, while others have the drainage hole low on the side of the pot.

WATERLOGGED CONTAINERS

If you notice that one of your pots is filled to the rim with water after a rain, the drain hole is blocked. Slowly rock the pot onto its side to let some of that water drain off. While the bottom of the pot is accessible, use a sturdy stick to unclog the drain hole—it's usually blocked by debris.

If the bottom of a pot was sitting flat on the paved surface, using pot feet (see opposite page) may be the solution. In some cases, the shrub in the pot has grown roots through the drainage hole. The rain makes the roots swell, blocking the drainage hole. There are several remedies, including breaking the pot and removing the plant. However, cutting the root with shears or a saw is also an option. In that case, just remove the plant and repot.

TYPES OF
Pots

Buying containers you will use around your home warrants careful selection. One of the perks of container gardens is that you can change the pots as your style, colors, or needs change, but it's always a good idea to start with pots you really like that are manufactured from materials that suit your needs. It will make planting them so much more rewarding. There are a wide variety of pots available, ranging from lightweight foam and fiberglass to terra-cotta and concrete. Consider the attributes of each to decide which style is best for you and your home.

LIGHTWEIGHT FOAM

If you are looking for pots that are portable or not too heavy for your deck or balcony, check these out. They are inexpensive yet resemble more costly containers. But be careful, they are not suited to tall, top-heavy plantings in areas where wind can blow them over, and they can break from freezing or close contact with a string trimmer.

GLAZED CERAMIC

These pots are largely imported, formed from clay, and fired hot enough to be durable. They are coated in colorful, glossy glazes that are a designer's dream for plants. Flowers come and go, but with these pots, there is always color. They are winter resistant in all but the Upper South (USDA Zones 5–6). Although not too expensive, you probably won't want to buy these every year. Thankfully they will last for years.

HYPERTUFA POTS

Inherently rustic and surprisingly durable, hypertufa is a mix of peat moss, perlite, and Portland cement that you can blend and make at home if you have a suitable mold. The resulting pots are durable, lighter than concrete ones, and are great for succulents and other plants. Many have the look of having been carved from volcanic rock.

FIBERGLASS

These pots are the great pretenders, mimicking other materials such as glazed ceramic, stone, wood, metal, or terra-cotta to perfection. They are both lightweight and durable, even in large sizes, and they often have plugs for their drainage holes so they can be used as a cachepot where moisture would be a problem for the surface below. When used as a decorative outer container, the inner, more utilitarian pot can be removed, watered, drained, and returned. Fiberglass pots range in price from moderate to expensive. They are unlikely to crack unless they receive a significant impact of some kind. You will be able to enjoy them for many years.

TERRA-COTTA

These pots have classic simplicity and are widely available. Terra-cotta is a porous material, so it absorbs moisture from the potting mix. Moisture then evaporates from the surface of the pot, and if the container is filled with plant roots, placed in the sun, or used in a dry climate, it can be a challenge for a gardener to keep the plants inside adequately watered. Over time, evaporation leaves a crust of fertilizer salts on the exterior. Likewise, moss will grow on pots that are constantly moist. Many consider this look of old greenhouse pots to be a lovely indication of age, while others prefer a clean look and scrub it away. Because it absorbs moisture, terra-cotta is notorious for cracking in winter due to the expansion of water in the clay as it freezes.

PLANTABLE BAGS

Lightweight but heavy-duty, these bags fold flat for easy storage and open up for big-time container gardening. While practical for anyone, they are outstanding for those with a weight limit on their balcony or too little off-season storage space. They are available in a variety of materials and colors, varying from burlap (not long term) to durable fabric that is breathable and reusable. Plants thrive in the breathable fabrics.

RESIN

These molded containers can be anything from streamlined, contemporary plastic to durable reproductions of classic terra-cotta. They have the advantage of being lightweight, an essential for gardens on balconies or decks. Many resin pots are designed to look like something they are not—terra-cotta, limestone, lead, etc. While the expectation may be that resin pots are inexpensive, large, well-designed ones are convenient, durable, and often equal in price to ceramic ones.

CAST STONE

Although these pots are cast in a mold from concrete mixed with natural and manufactured materials, they look convincingly like stone. The fine-grained texture resembling limestone is handsome and subsequently commands a handsome price. Designs such as *faux bois* benefit from the manufacturer's ability to incorporate stains that effectively mimic wood grain and tree bark. Known to be more durable than concrete, cast stone is a frequent choice for fine garden furnishings.

CONCRETE

Concrete containers are made from molds in countless styles. Some pots are more durable than others, owing to the mix of ingredients that vary by manufacturer, use of moisture sealants, and age. Concrete pots seem to improve in appearance over time, the surface growing green and mossy or darkening with accumulated debris in the recesses of their *bas-relief* designs, accentuating any patterns. Concrete pots may weaken over years of hot and cold weather accompanied by moisture.

WIRE WITH A COIR LINER

The classic hayrack hanging basket or window box is an ingenious way to raise your color off the ground. Although the price will vary depending on the width of your window, the cost is somewhat less than that of a custom window box. A hayrack offers a less formal style that many gardeners love. And it doesn't need to be limited to window dressing. Hang the flat-sided frame on blank walls or on the side of a deck from a sturdy railing or even from the fascia board. The liner is the expendable portion of this equipment, as it needs to be replaced about every other year. See page 94 for more information on hanging plants.

1 **2** **3**

HOW TO FIX CRACKS IN YOUR CONTAINERS

If the cracked pot is an inexpensive terra-cotta one, just recycle its broken shards over the drainage holes in future planted pots (see page 13). But if the crack is in a valued container, follow these directions for repair:

1. You'll need silicone caulk or adhesive, 12-gauge copper wire, and wire clippers to repair your pot.
2. When you see a crack developing in your concrete, stone, or terra-cotta container, use the silicone caulk on the inside of the pot.
3. Then, if appropriate for the damage and the value of the pot, use a twisted, 12-gauge copper wire around the pot where it will not slip off, usually under the rim. Think of it as a big twist tie. Tightening it will help support the damaged pot and give it many seasons of usefulness. Best of all, the copper wire is decorative, giving the container vintage appeal.

UNCOMMON CONTAINERS

Some of the most creative containers were never intended for growing plants. As long as it is sturdy enough to hold the weight of moist potting mix and a drainage hole can be added, then it can be used for planting. A wheelbarrow that now has a rusted hole in it can be filled with growing plants, as can washtubs, horse troughs, tire planters, old sinks, bathtubs, whisky barrels, garden boots, galvanized buckets, and plenty of other yard-sale finds. The only hesitation may be using iron urns, especially black ones, in full sun in a hot climate where they can get too hot. These are best placed in the shade.

Potting Mix

The bagged product that you buy is frequently called potting soil, but that's an incorrect description. Ideally there is no actual soil in the potting mix. Plants grow best in a medium that remains lightweight and loose through daily watering. The seemingly contradictory potting mix advice is that it needs to be moist but well drained. It must retain enough water to supply the plant with all that it needs, yet it should release the excess moisture so it will drain out of the pot. This allows air to fill the pore spaces so roots can have the oxygen they need for growth.

WHY GARDEN SOIL WON'T WORK

So why not just use soil from the garden? Garden soil, no matter how good it is, will compact in a container and hinder plant growth.

Southern soils vary widely from pure sand to pure clay, and most are a mixture, along with silt and organic matter. The component most easily lost is the organic matter, which is what keeps the soil loose and fertile. The South's hot summers hasten its breakdown, so compost, mulch, or both are frequently added to garden beds to maintain a suitable soil mix.

The same process happens in a pot, only when the organic matter is gone all that's left is an impenetrable block of the mineral components, which doesn't make plants' roots as happy as they would be in soil-free potting mix. Bagged potting mixes offer container gardeners the best chance of success.

Note: Bags sold at garden centers that are labeled "garden soil" may or may not contain actual soil. However, they are largely organic materials intended to enrich the soil in your garden, as opposed to supporting plant growth in a container.

WHAT'S IN POTTING MIX?

If there is no soil in potting mix, what's in it? The answer varies widely with brands. Generally, the staples of potting mix are Canadian sphagnum peat moss for holding moisture, aged pine bark and perlite (or vermiculite) to keep the mix fluffy, lime to raise the pH of the more acidic sphagnum peat moss, and fertilizer to nourish growing plants.

Usually a surfactant is included to make watering your pots more effective. Without it, the water runs through the dry mix and isn't readily absorbed. You may find other ingredients in the mix, such as sand, compost, Michigan peat, and polystyrene pellets, which are not always the best choice. In recent years, moisture-holding polymers have been added to potting mix, allowing it to hold more moisture without sacrificing its aeration.

While the fibrous, spongelike components in the mix physically anchor the plant and even hold nutrients to prevent them from washing out with the excess water, new additions may be biologically active as well. These include mycorrhizal fungi that occur naturally in undisturbed soils and boost the health of growing plants.

CAN YOU REUSE POTTING MIX?

Reusing potting mix is always tempting. But whether you reuse it or not is a judgment call. If a plant dies and the problem appears to be that the roots rotted (this is rare if the pot has drainage), then you definitely should not reuse the potting mix. When you remove plants from your pot, look at the remaining mix. Can you dig into it with your gloved fingers, or is it too compacted? Look at some of it in your hand. Is it crumbly with both small and large particles, or is it a dark homogeneous mass? If potting mix is old enough to be a compacted mass of muck, it has composted beyond its usefulness. Dump it into a garden bed, or use it to amend a planting hole in the garden. If the potting mix still looks like it did originally, mix it with some fresh potting mix to make it fluffy, and replant.

WHAT'S THE WHITE STUFF? ▶

The white pellets in potting mix are perlite, polystyrene, or both. You can tell the difference between the two because perlite is an expanded volcanic mineral that crunches when squeezed between your fingers; styrene bounces back. Perlite is added to potting mix to keep the mix fluffy and help with drainage. Styrene is a poor substitute because it floats, covering the surface of the potting mix with white dots. Ultimately, it can blow or wash out of the pot into nearby streams and keeps going. Mixes with or without perlite are preferable to mixes with polystyrene.

SINKING POTTING MIX

What do you do if the potting mix sinks and the plant is growing in only half of the pot? It's a common problem. You might think the soil is being lost through the drainage hole, and that could be part of the problem. Admittedly, potting mix is also made of decaying parts of formerly living plants: aged bark and sphagnum peat moss are primary ingredients. As plants grow, they build living tissue from the dead organic matter in the pot. So as plants grow and as potting mix ages and composts, these organic components disappear, making the mix in the pot shrink. If you want the plant to remain in the same pot, the first instinct is to add more potting mix to the top. Some plants will survive that, but it's best to remove the plant from the pot, shake as much old soil from the roots as possible, and then repot with fresh potting mix, raising the plant to a level just below the rim.

Plants

Now for the fun part! You've picked your pots and selected your potting mix. Let's dive into what goes in them.

PLANNING THE PLANT MIX

The popular way to think about the plants in a mixed pot is *thriller*, *filler*, and *spiller*. Mixing different plant forms allows each to have its own niche and not compete. Each has its place in the sun—or shade, as the case may be.

- **THE THRILLER** is a tall, upright, eye-catching plant that's for the center of the pot. Usually the thriller has a distinctive form or texture. Also, tall is subjective—the thriller should be tall *relative* to the other plants in the composition.
  EXAMPLES: papyrus, canna, elephant's ear, purple pennisetum, purple cordyline (pictured below), or tall fern
- **THE FILLER** visually anchors the taller thriller and fills in with a mounded form. The filler is the color mainstay, whether the source of color is from flowers or foliage.
  EXAMPLES: New Guinea impatiens, coleus (pictured below), geranium, variegated hosta, or heuchera
- **THE SPILLER** trails over the edge, partially obscuring the rim and outline of the pot. The spiller, more than the other players, gives the illusion of bounty, of abundance spilling from the pot. The spiller can be colorful, or it can subtly complement the other plants.
  EXAMPLES: miniature variegated English ivy, asparagus fern, begonia (pictured below), variegated sage (pictured below), lime green sweet potato vine (pictured at right), petunia or calibrachoa, or a showy form of Asiatic jasmine such as 'Summer Sunset' or 'Snow-N-Summer'

CONSIDER THE GROWTH RATE

When selecting plants, it's important to note how fast each one grows. If one grows a lot faster than the others, the container will either be out of balance or require a lot of pruning. If you fall in love with a particularly fast-growing plant, consider planting it in a container of its own and putting it in a grouping (see page 34).

READ LABELS

Since it's impossible to estimate how big a plant will grow by looking at it when it's a fresh, new plant at the nursery, you'll need to turn to the plant's label to guide you, particularly if it's a plant you're unfamiliar with. Ask for advice from the garden staff at the nursery, if needed. And keep in mind that in the long growing season of the South, well-adapted plants may grow larger than their labels indicate.

Purple cordyline

'Baby Wing Pink' begonia

'ColorBlaze Sedona' coleus

Variegated sage

THRILLER

A tall, upright, eye-catching plant that's for the center of the pot

FILLER

Anchors the taller thriller and fills in with a mounded form

SPILLER

Trails down over the edge, partially obscuring the rim and outline of the pot

Color

In container gardening, color is always the key ingredient, and the sources are varied. Flowers are usually the first thought for color, but foliage should not be overlooked. In fact, it should be the mainstay. It adds volume to the pot and nonstop color. While flowers add lovely shapes and pure charm, their blooms are fleeting.

CONSIDER THE COLOR WHEEL

While traditionally a tool for artists and designers, the color wheel can be helpful for gardeners, too. You can use it to assemble color combinations that you like, which you can then take to the garden store or nursery to use as a reference. When selecting the colors you want to use, consider these things:

- For a relaxed but refreshing look, consider colors that are adjacent to each other on the color wheel. This could be a blend of lavender, blue, and purple or shades of orange, coral, and pink. Mixing these colors creates a harmonious look that's also visually relaxing. Gardeners choosing to have a monochromatic color scheme, such as a white garden or blue garden, are actually choosing adjacent colors, even if that is not the intention.

- For a vibrant, energetic mix, look to colors that are opposites on the color wheel, such as coral and sky blue. The brighter the light in your home or garden, the more vivid the color should be to avoid appearing weak or washed out.

- For more complexity, select three colors that are equally spaced on the wheel, such as orange, violet, and green.

WARM AND COOL COLORS

Warm colors in the red to yellow range are considered more active and are more visible from a distance. Cool colors, ranging from purple to green, are more restful and aren't as visible from a distance.

THE COLOR WHEEL

While the color wheel doesn't need to be in your tool bucket alongside your clippers and gloves, it can help you visualize what color scheme pleases you most and will assist you in applying your preferences to your home. Snap a picture of this color wheel so it can be as close as your phone when you are shopping.

Lamb's Ears

'Nikko-Blue' French hydrangea

Hosta

Viola

'Mojito' elephant's ear

Purple Heart

Black-eyed Susan

Heuchera

Sun Coleus

'El Brighto' coleus

Bravo chrysanthemum

Oriental lily

MAINTAINING ORDER

Pyramidal and spherical forms, such as conifers and boxwood, are elements of formal garden design. While intentionally rigid and symmetrical, these shapes are oddly comforting. Perhaps it is deep in our genetic history that a cultivated landscape, rather than a wild and irregular one, feels safe. And with such elements, other beds can wax and wane with the seasons, yet the geometric forms maintain the order of the design.

Form

Including flowers and foliage with contrasting shapes and forms produces a container that is more visually appealing.

PLANNING THE CONTAINER DESIGN

The finished shape of a planted container is certainly easier to perceive after the plants are in place, but it is useful to think through the design in advance to have maximum impact in the setting. For example, a triangular plant design with the thriller tall in the middle, the filler to the outside of the doorway, and the spiller to the inside seems to point the way, almost like a host with an outstretched arm and open palm, inviting guests inside. This obtuse triangle could be reversed in the pot on the other side of the door for an attractive pairing.

CREATING AN APPEALING MIX ▶

FLOWERS—with their geometric spikes, disks, orbs, trumpets, and more—are even more interesting when different forms are combined. Consider how Shasta daisy would look with 'Icicle' Veronica. The rounded petals of the Shasta daisy form a beautiful contrast to the spiked Veronica.

FOLIAGE does more than support the flowers. It has an aesthetic role to play. Large leaves are bold and compelling, while narrow, grasslike leaves add energy to a composition. Combining narrow or finely divided leaves with large ones creates a contrast in texture. For example, variegated sweet flag (*Acorus gramineus* 'Variegatus') and Heuchera 'Electric Lime' combine linear foliage with round leaves. Even better, their growth habits combine an upright grower with a mounded one.

'Icicle' Veronica

Shasta daisy

A. gramineus 'Variegatus'

H. 'Electric Lime'

PLANTS WITH INTERESTING FORM

The form of a plant refers to the shape it takes as it grows.

- A mounded form (round outline) is typical of hosta, heuchera, cabbage and kale, geranium, boxwood, and some dwarf conifers.
- Upright plants grow straight up into a spike or a V shape. Examples include purple pennisetum grass, dwarf Alberta spruce, canna, or red hot poker.
- Trailing plants are those that cascade over the edge of a pot. You'll find prostrate rosemary, calibrachoa, creeping thyme, petunia, and miniature English ivy useful for this role.

Texture

Beyond the size of the plant and its form, the overall texture of each plant in a grouping will either amplify the appeal or diminish it. The size of the leaves and the pattern in which they grow all factor in. The important point to remember when combining foliage is that using a mix of different textures makes the grouping in the container more interesting.

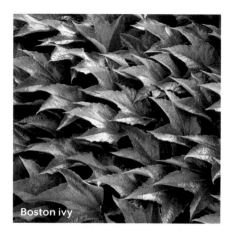

Boston ivy

Hosta

PATTERN BECOMES TEXTURE

A good example of pattern is a fern. The leaflets are large or small, depending upon what kind of fern you choose, but it is the arrangement of the leaflets in a regular, repeating pattern that gives the plant its texture. Other examples of pattern include the whorled leaves of a hosta, or the fish-scale pattern of Boston ivy on a wall.

For example, a 'Macho' fern (*Nephrolepis biserrata,* pictured at right) with its large leaflets and long fronds will be a coarse texture in a pot next to a boxwood because the pattern of the fern's foliage is bolder. However, planted next to a big-leaved fatsia (*Fatsia japonica,* pictured at right), it will be a finer texture. Both of these monochromatic combinations are interesting because the texture within the plant pairing is different. The labels "coarse" and "fine" are simply the mental vocabulary used when selecting plants to be captivating neighbors.

N. biserrata 'Macho'

F. japonica

CONTAINER RECIPE

1. 'Maui Gold' elephant's ear (*Colocasia esculenta* 'Maui Gold')
2. Persian shield (*Strobilanthes dyerianus*)
3. Orange SunPatiens
4. Citronella (*Pelargonium citrosum*)
5. Angel vine (*Muehlenbeckia complexa*)

Foliage

Foliage can be a constant source of color with minimal effort. Foliage can also serve to bring out the colors in your flowers. Begin by determining the size of your pot and the light exposure it will have. Then select plants that will fit into the pot, allowing a little extra growing room.

CONTAINER RECIPE

1. 'Wasabi' coleus
2. Cast-iron plant
3. 'Pink Beauty' caladium
4. Variegated Algerian ivy
5. Asparagus fern

GREEN

RED

PURPLE

BROWN

Erythrina variegata

Acalypha wilkesiana 'Inferno'

Acalypha wilkesiana 'Kona Coast'

'Trailing Red' coleus

Manihot esculenta 'Variegata'

Acalypha wilkesiana 'Musaica'

Setaria palmifolia 'Rubra Variegata'

'Beckwith's Gem' coleus

Persian Shield

Musa 'Siam Ruby'

Alternanthera dentata 'Purple Knight'

'Smallwood's Driveway' coleus

MAKE FOLIAGE COUNT

To create beautiful containers with foliage, start by selecting a favorite foliage plant. Then, choose another that contrasts with the first. Finally, add a flower or final foliage plant that complements the other two. Be sure the plants enjoy the same sort of light and soil conditions. The ones shown here are good starting points.

PLANTING YOUR
Containers

You have chosen your plant combination.
Your pot is in place with potting mix. Now it's time to put
them all together. Start with the tall and move to the filler
and then the trailing. 1.2.3. and you're done!

HOW TO PLANT CONTAINERS

1. Partially fill your pot with potting mix, and arrange your plants, still in their pots. They will probably have been grown in pots of different sizes, so dig down or mound up potting mix so that the surface of the root mass of each of the plants is at the same level as its neighbors. That level should be about an inch below the rim of the pot.
2. When you are satisfied with the placement, carefully remove the individual pots, loosen encircling roots, set the plants in place, and fill between them with potting mix. Water thoroughly.

COLD-WEATHER CONTAINERS

In areas with a hard winter, planting in fall is more successful with plants of more mature size. If you have a choice between a cell pack of 4 to 6 pansies or one in a 4-inch pot, the larger, 4-inch pansy pot is more likely to survive winter and bloom more. Certainly, the same is true for other plants, especially in a container where they will be more exposed to the cold than if planted in the ground. They will not have long to grow before winter, and they need to be large enough to handle the cold weather, assuming you have chosen hardy plants.

CONTAINER ALL-STARS

We recommend these annuals and perennials for their color, ease of use, and versatility.

Autumn fern: Perennial, Shade

Dragon wing Begonia: Annual, Shade or Partial Sun

Hibiscus: Annual, Sun

Caladium: Annual, Shade or Sun

Impatiens: Annual, Shade or Sun

Hosta: Perennial, Shade

Coleus: Annual, Shade or Sun

Succulents: Perennial, Partial Shade or Sun

Petunia: Annual, Sun

Viola: Annual, Sun

Heuchera: Perennial, Shade or Partial Shade

Lantana: Annual, Sun

CONTAINER RECIPE

1. 'Florida Sweetheart' caladiums
2. 'Celebration' caladiums
3. White wishbone flower
4. Golden creeping Jenny

Location

The location of the pots is a key consideration in container gardening. Beyond the amount of light that falls on the pot and its proximity to water, there are a few other things to consider.

PLACEMENT

A lot depends on how the pot will be viewed. If it is pressed against a wall or hedge, there's no need to plant it to be equal on all sides. It should have a distinct front and back—tall plants should be pushed to the back and shorter ones can stair-step down toward the viewer. If a pot is located in the center of a garden bed or patio and is to be viewed from all sides, it is customary for the tall plant to be in the center with progressively shorter ones positioned toward the rim.

HEIGHT OF THE CONTAINER

The angle of view will also determine how a pot is planted. If the pot is positioned at or above eye level, it's important for the planting to be full, colorful, and overflowing for close-up viewing. Looking down on a pot means that every detail should be eye-catching from above—whether it's planted with a single plant or a mixture. The surface of the potting mix should be mulched (see page 48) to avoid an unfinished appearance.

◄ DISTANCE MATTERS

If the container is positioned as a distant focal point, bright colors, big leaves, or a sculptural form are needed to command attention. For example, a golden- or black-leaved elephant's ear or an agave in an urn functions as a living sculpture. A bird of paradise adds height, as well as large leaves, for a strong statement. For pots that are set near at hand, for example beside a bench or door, details matter most, including variegated or ruffled leaves, textural contrasts, and color echoes.

ARRANGING YOUR
Containers

Grouping pots can make your garden look like a visual feast, the outdoor equivalent of a dessert buffet. With a little planning, collections of pots can have a striking impact in the landscape. The key is to plant the pots and arrange them with the ultimate design in mind.

GO WITH A GROUP ▶

You may find that the plants perform better in a group of pots rather than planted all together in one. If you have an established shrub or small tree that has filled the potting mix with roots, leaving no room for seasonal color, add companion pots to meet that need.

Sometimes a pot, or a pair of pots, seems inadequate. The space may be too large for a solo pot to fill it, or you may not want to invest in a pot large enough for the scale of the setting. Don't worry; just use several.

CONTAINER GROUPING TIPS

There are no specific rules to follow, only guidelines to consider:

- A group of pots may hold the same thriller, filler, and spiller (see page 20) that would grow in one pot. Just use a pot for each and arrange.
- If one or two of the plants are evergreen, they can remain in their pots for several seasons. You will not need to disturb them every time you change the seasonal color. It is more economical in terms of time and materials to simply change the seasonal color in one pot.

- ▶ You can use all one material, such as terra-cotta, in your grouping or use a mix of pots in varying forms, sizes, and materials to create a complementary collection.
- ▶ Variation in sizes and elevations helps create a pleasing composition. If pots are grouped on multiple steps of a staircase, they are naturally staged. However, pots placed in a group on a level surface will need to have different widths and heights. Tall urns, low bowls, and standard-size pots combine to keep each in easy view.
- ▼ Odd numbers are easier to arrange. Containers in a group of three, five, or even seven come together in a configuration with natural balance. Sometimes one of the group can be something other than a pot, such as a sphere or a pumpkin.

- Raising a pot can help create a satisfying composition. A pedestal or a plinth is always handy to make a tall container out of a shorter one. Sometimes you just don't have the right pot, but you may have extra ones. Turn a sturdy pot upside down, and place the planted one on top of it. If the proportions are right, it will look great. You can also put a trio of bricks beneath the pot to raise it a few inches. In both of these cases, the staging is usually hidden, at least partially, by other pots in the foreground or to the side.
- Plant and maintain some pots to be universal members of a group. Think of them as the backup singers in a band. For example, a rounded golden conifer or a pot of autumn fern, heuchera, or lamb's ears will live from one season to the next and be versatile enough to fit with many different combinations of plants in a group of pots. They are not the standout in the composition, but they are reliable members of whatever grouping you assemble next.

BREAKING THE
"Rules"

Although the rule of thumb is to have a thriller, filler, and spiller, not all pots must feature three kinds of plants. There can be many more plants in a composition, especially if the pot is large. Other times, there may be only one plant or multiples of one kind of plant. Plant with originality and respond to the situation at hand, regardless of the rules, for inspired results. Here are a few examples.

BREAK OUT OF THE THRILLER-SPILLER-FILLER MOLD

Pots viewed from all sides or those planted for a geometric effect can have a central feature plant (thriller) and a skirt of a second (filler or spiller). Sometimes you just need a big mass of color, and if the plant grows large, it does not need companions. Hosta is particularly effective used alone in a pot. The leaves become a big whorl of green.

KEEP IT LOW ▶

Low-growing plants can go solo in a pot. Examples include succulents that grow in a mat or rosette form, as well as trailing plants such as verbena or trailing pansy. Even a blue ground-hugging juniper can be more than just a voice in the choir. Frequently taller plants overshadow them, both visually and culturally.

◄ USE TRANSPLANTS FOR SHORT-TERM POTS

When creating a container for an event or special occasion, setting an abundance of transplants into a container is the way to go. Of course, they cannot succeed in such an overplanted arrangement. Enjoy them for the party, and then move them into their summer homes in the garden.

◄ CLUSTER POTS FOR BIG IMPACT

Group pots and plant them all the same to create a large mass. This arrangement gives the appearance of abundance and provides impact, especially from a distance.

USE SIMILAR COLORS

Choose flowers and foliage that are the same or have similar colors for a strong, cohesive design. You can use repetition to your advantage by restricting your colors and having them mirror the surroundings.

Repetition

Use repetition to make a mixed container or a group of containers cohesive. Repeat the yellow of a glazed pot in the yellow flowers of lantana, or echo a blue door with blue flowers.

REPEATING ELEMENTS ▶

You can also repeat an element between different pots in a group to unify the arrangement. For example, the same pink tulips can be used in different pots, even if the other plants used in the containers are different. Or you can repeat a plant from a container in the soil nearby, as if it has reseeded. This instantly makes the container appear to be a long-term resident of the garden. Likewise, you can echo an element from the garden in the pot.

QUICK
Containers

Knowing *why* you are planting pots will help you decide *how* to plant them. For most containers, buy young plants, set them in the pots (see page 30), water, and watch them grow. They will surprise and reward you with their fast growth, but sometimes it isn't quick enough.

CONTAINER RECIPE

1. Dwarf arborvitae
2. Zinnia
3. Autumn fern
4. Petunia
5. Ivy

PLANT FOR QUICK IMPACT

If it is spring and you are having an event in your garden in a few weeks, the priority is planting for quick impact. You will want the pots to look full and beautiful immediately. Plan to set full-sized plants in the pot at least two days prior to the event. This allows just enough time for the plants to settle into place and for leaves to turn toward the sun. They will look as if they grew that way.

INSTANT IMPACT

If you need beautiful containers that look as if they've been planted for awhile, follow these steps:

1. Place the pots you have chosen where you want them to be. They're lighter and easier to move when they're empty.

2. Fill them halfway with a quality potting mix, but keep the bag nearby.

3. Use a fully-grown hanging basket to give each planter the look of instant maturity. It is the only way to get plants trailing like they would if they had been growing for two months, rather than two days. Depending on the type of plant you are using, you can use one of two methods. For fragile or brittle plants such as a begonia, carefully remove the wire or plastic hanger, slip the plant from the remaining pot, and set it in the container, minimizing breakage of those brittle stems.

4. Another technique is to use a more forgiving plant such as an asparagus fern, English ivy, geranium, angel vine, or calibrachoa in a hanging basket. Do the same as above, but once you get the plant out of its plastic pot, look for the location of the several plants the grower used to create fullness in the hanging basket.

5. Carefully pull or cut the root mass apart between the small plants. The result is two, half round pieces that work well for a pair of pots. Plants grown in hanging baskets have the maturity to instantly trail over the edge of a container.

6. Fill the gaps in the potting mix and water well. Do this far enough in advance to give the new planting a couple of days to recover from the transplanting. It will look as if it had been growing there for weeks.

Gearing Up

Just like the kitchen is a work area for food prep, the potting bench is a work area for gardening, and specifically container gardening. This is also the place where you can divide perennials, take cuttings, and start seeds, all while standing up straight and saving your back.

POTTING BENCH ESSENTIALS

- An uncluttered area where you have room to work enables you to walk up and get started. If you are working on large pots, set them on a low bench or on top of a sturdy, empty pot that has been turned upside down.

- A watering can or two can be helpful. It is so much easier to apply life-saving moisture on a hot day if you have a watering can than it is to stretch out the hose and put it back again. Just keep them filled with water and ready to use. If you use them regularly, mosquitoes will not have time to hatch.

- If you find open bags of potting mix unsightly and potentially messy, consider a lidded trash can that will hold your bag. It will sit inconspicuously beside your bench, and your mix will always be dry. Besides, if you leave a bag open, an enterprising bird (usually a Carolina wren) will make a nest in it, sending you back to the garden center for more to avoid disturbing the little family.

▶ A water source is a must for settling freshly potted plants into their new homes. The next best thing to a garden hose that will go the distance is an outdoor sink. It is ideal for newly potted plants. The drain water does not need to go into the septic system or sewer; the runoff can be piped to water plants.

- Fertilizer is always helpful, especially in the form of timed-release granules that will feed each time you water, as well as a product to be used in a hose-end sprayer for a quick fix when plants need a boost.

- The most important piece of equipment for a container gardener is a hand truck and bungee cords for moving unwieldy pots in and out of place. It also helps to have a second pair of hands to help. Tip: If you forget to put the pot in place before you plant, get help and use a commercially available device called a pot lifter to carry it to its destination. Water it well once you have it in place.

SMALL TOOLS

- Keep labels and a no. 2 pencil on hand to quickly tag a plant, especially if you are gifting it.
- Garden gloves take a lot of pain out of gardening. They are especially important when working with potting mix that contains sphagnum peat moss (also thorny roses, hay, and soil) to prevent a fungal infection in a torn cuticle or other open wound. Many types are washable, especially the knitted ones with waterproof palms and fingers. Keep several pairs on hand so you can toss them in the laundry after a day in the garden. Just wash them and put them back on the potting bench to dry.
- Insect repellent, bandage strips, and first aid spray are good additions to save steps and time. You will inevitably need them.

▲ Hand tools should be, well, on hand. Small clippers or florist's snips are ideal for cutting small material, as you would when deadheading basil, coleus, zinnias, and more. In addition, an old kitchen knife is handy for dividing root-bound plants or releasing a stubborn transplant from its pot. Utility scissors are great for opening bags of potting mix and such. Finally, it never hurts to have a trowel nearby. You may want to dig up a piece of hosta, thyme, creeping Jenny, or other established garden plant for a quick addition to a mixed container.

- A nailbrush, soap, and hand cream are as much a luxury after working in the garden as they are a necessity, especially if you have an outdoor sink.

Designing
AS YOU SHOP

Typically garden centers and nurseries separate their plants into groups such as trees, shrubs, perennials, tropicals, and annuals. It can be advantageous to browse areas and types of plants that you don't normally consider for your containers. Have you shopped in the shrub or ground cover areas? Sometimes the more original and pleasing combinations result from selecting plants from different sections of the garden center.

CONSIDER TROPICAL PLANTS

For tropical plants in a mixed container, look to a tall angel-wing begonia paired with trailing and spreading philodendron. A tropical palm or aralia will provide height as well as screening. Peace lily (*Spathiphyllum* sp.) and anthurium contribute blooms as well as foliage, and dracaena offers color from its variegated foliage. In addition, the tropical nature of these plants makes the summer garden in a temperate climate all the more inviting.

OPT FOR A NATURAL LOOK

For naturalistic touches, consider ground covers. A single, small pot of variegated monkey grass (*Liriope* sp.) or sweet flag (*Acorus* sp.) will add linear foliage that gives a punch of energy to most containers. Monkey grass will also put up welcome spikes of blue flowers in August.

◀ THINK OUTSIDE THE BOX

It may help to think of container gardening like flower arranging—you can put plants together that don't normally coexist. For example, combine an evergreen arborvitae from the shrub section with pansies from the bedding plants and variegated ivy from houseplants or ground covers. Flowering shrubs such as hydrangea, tropical foliage such as bird of paradise, or hardy evergreens such as gardenia or camellia will lend welcome height to a container. The possibilities are as varied as the selection at your local nursery. Even if the plant you buy will grow too large for the pot, don't worry. You can move it to your garden when it needs more room or when you are ready for a change.

Caladium

Hosta

Aspidistra

Polka dot plant

REFRESH YOUR SHADED CONTAINERS

Sometimes shaded containers need to be more than just caladiums, coleus, and impatiens to keep the pots looking fresh and original. Most tropical foliage plants are grown under shade so that they will adapt to life indoors, the most common destination for them. This means that they will adjust readily to life in a container on the north or east side of your home, under a porch overhang, or on a patio under a canopy of tall trees.

Shade-loving, temperate perennials such as aspidistra, heuchera, hosta, and autumn fern are workhorse plants in a pot with double-flowered impatiens, wishbone flower (*Torenia* sp.), Rieger begonia, caladium, and polka dot plant (*Hypoestes* sp.). They help give the appearance of a garden in a pot, rather than just a dollop of color.

Double-flowered impatiens

Rieger begonia

Heuchera

Wishbone flower

Watering

By spending just a little time each week on your containers, you can keep your potted plants looking their very best.

THE IDEAL WAY TO WATER

Container plants need water, and in hot weather, they need it every day. The keys to making watering as painless as possible are to have good tools and to be prepared.

The ideal way to water is with a gentle spray. A nozzle that looks like a showerhead is called a breaker, presumably because it breaks the flow of water in the hose into dozens of streams that fall without injuring the plant, like a gentle rain.

Water an average-size pot for about 20 seconds—that seems like a long time when you are standing there on a hot afternoon. The pot may fill with water and overflow because the potting mix cannot drain fast enough. Just let it soak in while you are watering other plants, and then water it again. Be sure that all of the potting mix is wet with no dry pockets. If in doubt, water it several times. You may see bubbles coming out of the mix as water displaces the air in the pore spaces. That's good. After you stop watering, the excess will flow out through the drainage hole. The vacuum created by the water exiting the pot pulls fresh air into the mix. The benefit of this is twofold: moisture and oxygen for roots.

THE BEST WATERING TOOLS ▶

It's worth it to invest in updated watering tools, including a wand, adjustable head, and flexible hose. Watering wands are helpful for reaching hanging baskets and are efficient because they get the water right where it needs to go. They are available in different lengths; you can find them with 16-, 24-, 30-, 36-, or even 48-inch wands. If you are watering in a tight space, a 16-inch wand may be all that you need. If you need to reach tall hanging baskets or a thirsty plant deep in a bed, choose a longer wand.

Wands can also regulate the flow of water, which is helpful with new plants that can't handle a strong spray of water. Flexible hoses are lightweight and easy to maneuver around your yard.

WILTING PLANTS?

If you know from past experience that your pots will wilt before you get home in the afternoon, consider two possibilities. The first is that the roots just cannot keep up with the needs of the leaves due to heat, even though there is moisture in the soil. You know this is the case if the leaves perk up again as soon as the sun and temperature go down.

The second possibility is that the plants have matured, filled the pot with roots, and the potting mix just cannot hold as much water as is needed for a hot day. In this case, move the pots to a spot with a little afternoon shade as a temporary solution for the season.

Then in the future, add some moisture-holding polymers to the mix before you plant. These crystals are about the same as the crystals in baby diapers that are superabsorbent.

Using the recommended amount on the label, stir moisture-holding polymers into the potting mix in the lower two-thirds of the pot, so you will not see the gelatinous blobs that they become once fully expanded. That is also the ideal location for them to release extra moisture to the roots. Then finish filling the pot with potting mix without any polymers added.

If your potting mix says it already has moisture holding polymers in it but you don't see anything, don't worry. The particles are very small, and you likely will not be able to see them. You can add a little more, but it should be less than you would add if there were none in the mix. If you add too much, you will know it. The moisture-holding polymers will swell and push up—the only direction that the potting mix can go. If you really overdo it, the plants will be uprooted by the expanding mix and be pushed out of the pot.

When watering a dry, wilted plant in a pot, spray the foliage as well as pour water onto the dry potting mix. If the potting mix has pulled away from the sides of the pot, the first water will probably go around the dry mass rather than being absorbed by it. If you don't make progress getting the potting mix to rehydrate after two or three attempts, get a saucer and let the pot sit in an inch of water until it is gone. The mix will slowly absorb the water like a dry sponge. Then remove the saucer, and water the plant again to be sure it is thoroughly moist.

AUTOMATIC IRRIGATION

For those who travel frequently or have a second home, automatic irrigation may be a good option to help keep your containers healthy. It can be part of a larger system or freestanding. Ask an irrigation professional to assist you with the right system for your needs.

Grooming

Keeping containers looking their best requires grooming. Take a snip here and there to remove a dead flower or an errant branch. (Petunias in particular benefit from being cut back by a third to a half of their size when they get long and stringy.) Always fertilize afterwards. Pruning can also help restore the balance in a mixed container where one plant has overtaken another.

CONTROLLING WEEDS

Surprisingly, weeds can sprout in pots. Frequently they're from a cache of seeds stashed in the soft potting mix by chipmunks. Often these are sunflower seeds from the bird feeder, but occasionally it is an acorn, sprouting into a young oak tree. Pull them all before they get too large to remove.

MULCHING CONTAINERS ▶

One of the best ways to ease maintenance is to mulch containers. It may seem odd, but mulch does the same thing in a pot that it does in the garden. It insulates the soil from heat, it slows drying, and it minimizes weeds. However, you can have much more fun with the mulch when gardening in a pot. It can be a standard soil conditioner made of finely ground pine bark, but it can also be decorative stone pebbles, glass gravel, crystals, fossils, or whatever your creative mind imagines. Pinecones make excellent mulch, particularly if your favorite feline has found your pot to be a handy bed or litter box.

CHOOSING A FERTILIZER

Growing plants need nutrients. Plants growing in a container cannot forage beyond the pot to find what they need, so they are essentially living on an island of potting mix. Some of the nutrients that plants need to grow can be washed out of the pot with frequent watering, so plants will need your help to survive.

Most premium potting mixes will have some fertilizer included. Just look on the label to know for sure. For the most part, it lasts about two weeks, just enough to get your plants growing. After that, it is up to you.

- Use a **soluble fertilizer** in a watering can or hose-end sprayer to nurture your garden. Mix according to the label directions. Use it to water your pots about once every two weeks. That includes spraying it on the foliage. Leaves can take in the nutrients as well as the roots.

- Gardeners who are short on time will enjoy the convenience of **timed-release granules** (see photo below right). These are the little green, blue, or tan beads that you have probably seen on the soil surface of potted plants in nurseries. They actually release a little fertilizer every time you water. If you see them in the pot, don't assume that they are enough. Squeeze one between your thumb and forefinger. If it crushes and is empty, it is spent. You need to add more. Read the label on the product you buy. It will tell you how long it will last in weeks or months. Adjust your application by the growth that you observe. If it is a 3- to 4-month product and growth seems to have slowed after 10 weeks, it may be time to apply more. Hot weather can cause the granules to release more quickly than indicated on the label. Your plant may need a boost in the latter weeks of summer and fall.

TIME FOR A
Change

When the season is changing and you know that at least some
of your container plants will succumb to temperatures too hot or too cold,
it's time to make a decision. When should you change the plantings,
and when you do, can you reuse some of the plants in your pot?

GETTING THE TIMING RIGHT ▶

Summer plantings perform best if they can get started before the weather gets too hot, so make plans to change out your containers several weeks after the last spring frost, which is when all the summer annuals arrive at the garden center anyway.

Containers and window boxes for fall and winter are best planted while the weather is mild and plants are still growing, which allows their roots to spread out into the new potting mix. While some summer annuals look tired by that time, many do not. You may be pulling them out before they decline. Think of your plants as if they were athletes who retire at the peak of their careers. They will never look bad, and neither will your pots.

LEARN PLANT LINGO

Here are some helpful definitions and descriptions to guide you when you're selecting plants.

- **Annuals** must change with the season. It doesn't take more than one year of gardening to learn that begonias, caladiums, coleus, marigolds, sweet potatoes, and such do not like freezing. Tropical foliage plants (houseplants) are either annuals or hardy perennials, depending on where you live and garden. If you live where winter seldom brings freezes, your biggest problem is a plant's tendency to outgrow its pot. However, for those who garden where winter means freezing temperatures, they are gratifying annuals to grow indoors.

  It's difficult to toss out plants that still look nice (like anthurium, Rex begonia, Chinese evergreen, snake plant, or bird's nest fern) simply because it's time to rotate the plantings in your pot. If you have room, repot them for use indoors, to hold through winter in a home greenhouse or heated garage, or gift them to someone who will enjoy them.

- **Perennial plants** are outstanding in containers, but you want to choose the ones that remain showy for the entire season, if not the entire year. However, perennials that are not evergreen will leave a container looking sad and empty in winter. You will want to have something interesting in the pot for winter, provided your pot is frost proof. Move these perennials to the garden or to an out-of-the-way area where you can hold them over and reuse them in your spring and summer pots.

  Autumn fern and heuchera look great year-round in all but the coldest zones. Hosta and heuchera are good examples of plants that thrive in a container, even where they sometimes fail in the soil of Deep South gardens. In a container, hosta will be protected from the voles and slugs that plague it, and if it is on your deck, the deer will not get it either.

- **Woody plants** (trees and shrubs) will grow more lovely with time up to a point—the point at which they become too large or the potting mix too degraded to support them. For example, you could have a cascading 'Crimson Queen' Japanese maple in a pot that is a bare stick with a few

PROTECTING YOUR POTS

Of course there is the matter of actually maintaining the pot itself. Any material that is porous will absorb water and then shatter during freezing weather. These pots are best brought inside so they do not freeze, or empty them, turn them upside down, and store them where they will not be exposed to rain or snow.

branches in its first season, but it will grow into a full, feathery masterpiece in three years. Its roots will fill a large pot to the point that there is little room to add seasonal color. Until you tire of it—or it begins to decline—do not worry about planting color around it in the pot. Allow the bare branches to be what they are, bare winter branches with a pretty habit. Add color in a second or third pot, if needed (see Go with a Group, page 34). If you prefer evergreens, consider agarista, boxwood, camellia, fatsia, and many of the dwarf conifers to give you green all year long.

CONTAINERS ON ROTATION

Pots make a beautiful accent on porches and even in the garden. Depending on the size of the pot, rotate containers inside the house to the outdoors through the changing seasons for continual interest.

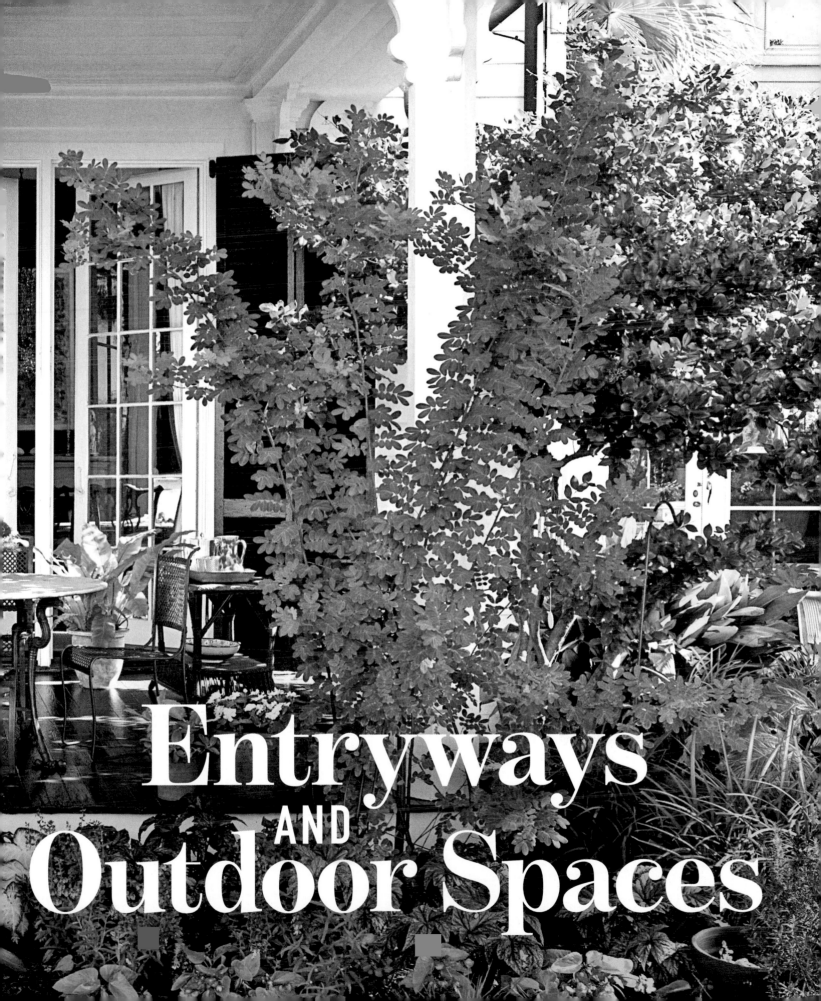

Entryways
AND
Outdoor Spaces

CREATE A WELCOMING
Outdoor Space

Thoughtfully chosen, sited, and planted, containers have a presence that delights and make the outdoors feel as much like a part of the home as the indoors.

USING CONTAINERS OUTDOORS

They can define the boundaries of an outdoor room and emphasize the seating area, entry, or stairs. Containers can also be decorative, bringing color to areas that could not be planted otherwise. Aside from pots by the door, containers allow you to plant on concrete, brick, decking, or any surface that cannot be cultivated. They may fill a void in an out-of-the-way corner, transforming it from unused to enjoyed.

Whether they serve to say welcome, frame an entrance or view, provide a focal point, anchor every window with a planted box, hang from the eaves, or soften an otherwise sterile, paved outdoor room, containers make any outdoor space feel like someone is at home and that they care. Planted containers make life outdoors, as well as the view from indoors, a lot nicer than it would be otherwise. Here are some general tips as you start thinking about using containers in your outdoor space.

◄ CHOOSE A LARGE CONTAINER

Bigger containers may be appropriate for the scale of your space (see page 58) but they also give plants plenty of room to take root. Pots are only too large when they become an obstacle to walking into the house. When an extra-large pot is needed, it's a pleasure to work with. Whether you select a tree, shrub, or summer bedding plants, these arrangements seldom look healthier. That's because larger pots hold more potting mix, and plants in gardens rarely have such ideal growing conditions.

CONTAINER RECIPE

1. 'Silver Falls' dichondra
2. Million bells

CHOOSE A PALETTE

When choosing flowers and foliage for your entryway or outside, start
by shopping for plants in colors that enhance the exterior of your home.
Soft, light shades can feel feminine and romantic, while bright colors
shout welcome in a cheerful, friendly way (see page 22). Nature-inspired
shades, such as green and brown, are best used as fillers and to help the
brighter colors in your containers pop. If you're a traditionalist, try a classic
combination such as red and white. If you like a more modern look, try a
simple monochromatic scheme (see page 76).

Also, look at the colors of your home—the bricks or siding, the trim,
the door. Don't overlook the surface of the walkway or porch where the
container will be placed. Are there plants with seasonal color nearby?
These are your references when you are shopping, so take your snapshots
with you.

CONTAINER RECIPE

1. 'Caliente Dark Rose' geranium
2. 'Fireworks' pennisetum
3. 'Sweet Georgia Heart Red' sweet potato vine
4. 'Easy Wave Pink' petunia
5. 'AngelMist Spreading Pink' angelonia

◄ SELECT THE PLANTS

Be sure to choose flowers and foliage that have the same light, moisture, and temperature needs. Combine annuals and perennials of different textures, height, forms, and bloom types for the most visual appeal. Practice the *thriller, filler, spiller* formula to create beautiful and visually interesting containers (see page 20).

CONTAINER RECIPE

1. 'The Flume' coleus
2. 'Supertunia Vista Bubblegum' petunia
3. 'Angelface Pink' angelonia
4. 'Supertunia Sangria Charm' petunia
5. 'Dolce Blackcurrant' heuchera

GROUP FOR IMPACT ▲

If the area is large and your pots are small, consider grouping several containers instead of using just one large one. You can try whatever assortment you like and keep the plantings colorful or try a monochromatic scheme (see page 76). If in doubt, choose a larger container or group of containers. If too small, the containers appear like someone tried, but didn't quite achieve the goal.

REMEMBER OFTEN OVERLOOKED SPACES ▶

Take a look at your deck, balcony, patio, porch, pool, walkway, and steps. Are there places that need a container or two to appear furnished and welcoming? A bright, lush container at the end of a deck or dock serves as a beautiful boundary, preventing missteps.

DESIGN TO
Scale

Larger spaces call for bigger containers. If the pot is too small for the space, it will always look underscaled—nothing you plant in it will make it look grander, so go bold right from the start.

HEIGHT CONSIDERATIONS ▶

Pots raise plants to heights they could not otherwise attain, lending importance to a plant by giving it a pedestal. They provide instantaneous impact that might otherwise require seasons of growth. And sometimes a space needs containers that can provide vertical heft to fill the visual space, adding a wow factor from a distance.

◀ PLANT PROPORTIONALLY

Containers are like vases: The flowers need to be in proportion to the pot. Having tall plants as well as trailing ones helps balance large containers and urns.

MAKING A STATEMENT IN A SMALLER AREA ▼

If there isn't room for a big pot by your door, consider a tall slender container to provide mass on a smaller footprint. A narrow space needs a narrow pot, but that doesn't mean it needs to be small. Go tall.

CONTAINER RECIPE

1. 'Garden White' caladium
2. 'Baby Wing Pink' begonia
3. 'Evergold' carex
4. Silver waffle plant

CONTAINER RECIPE

1. Upright elephant's ear
2. Red-leaved ti plant
3. 'Little Ruby' alternanthera

CREATING COLORFUL CONTAINERS

To create bright casual pots, look for plant and flower combinations that add a variety of color. Start with an evergreen anchor like boxwood or holly, and then add in color. For height and mounding color, use zinnias, angelonia, impatiens, vinca, or petunia. For traling plants, try sweet potato vine or Cuban oregano.

CHOOSE THE RIGHT CONTAINER

The link between the house and the pot begins with the container itself, which is then enhanced by the plants. Classical designs with garlands, lions' heads, and even rustic faux bois recall a romantic past. Simplified, sleek, or colorful planters have a more avant-garde appeal suited to contemporary and playful garden scenes. In addition, containers made from repurposed objects such as former washbasins, animal troughs, and even leaky birdbaths allow the gardener to bring creativity and a sense of antiquity to the garden.

CONSIDER THE STYLE OF YOUR HOME ▶

Welcome pots extend from the home to the yard. Some architectural styles need only the graphic element of a single, perfectly scaled pot set asymmetrically to accent the door. More traditional homes may call for a pair of pots to be symmetrically placed and planted. Placing containers is key. Here, white planter boxes flanking the walk lead you to the front door and lend a more formal, symmetrical look. Because the galvanized buckets aren't the same height, they'd look odd flanking the door. Positioning them to one side concentrates the color.

WELL-SUITED PLANTS

When it's time to plant, remember that evergreen shrubs, especially geometrically shaped ones, are a good choice for traditional architecture. For a less formal, cottage-garden style, use a planting of mixed flowers and foliage in a large container, a group of pots, or window boxes to give the house a more spontaneous, carefree appearance.

FRAMING AN
Entrance

Planting fresh, colorful pots by your front door is the simplest and most appealing way to say welcome. These beautiful containers wordlessly draw guests in as if to say, "You're going to like it here."

DRESS UP THE
Porch

Create an inviting room on your porch just like you would do inside your home. Lush and vibrant pots are the accessories to a porch that will draw you and your family to this outdoor space.

◄ CREATE A SOPHISTICATED SPACE

Understated sophistication can be achieved through repetition of similar shaped pots and plants. Here, there are urns used throughout the space that each have a similar patina creating cohesion. Also, by focusing the color palette and using only green plants in the containers along the edge of the seating area, the variety of textures really stand out. The seasonal centerpiece offers a pop of color that can easily be changed depending on time of year.

GIVE YOUR PORCH A CASUAL LOOK ►

A porch can also be an opportunity to create a lively living space. Using bright annuals helps give this space a fun casual vibe that's also welcoming. The brightly colored flowers used in the pots complement the outdoor pillows; planting the vibrant zinnias, vinca, petunias, angelonia, and other annuals in containers makes them stand out while still giving the space a unified look.

GO BOLD

Containers are an opportunity for you to go bold. Here, the furniture and pots are all neutral colors and wood tones that never go out of style—it's a background that allows the colorful plants to shine.

REPEAT COLORS WHEN POSSIBLE

Whether it's an entryway or a back porch, any area near your home can look inviting with a few simple tips. When picking containers, repeat the same colors and/or materials if possible. The pots can also coordinate with any of the furniture that's being used. Seen above, this hardworking entryway is utilitarian but also inviting because of the soothing green plants, little pops of colorful flowers, and repetition of similar-colored materials.

CONSIDER THE CORNERS ▶

Corners can be a great opportunity to fill with an interesting accent pot. A trellis with an annual or perennial vine provides visual interest with its height in this seating nook. Depending on sun and watering demands, there are several vines, such as clematis, jasmine, moon vine, and hyacinth bean vine, that make attractive additions to a potted trellis.

CONTAINER RECIPE

1. Asparagus fern
2. Ornamental oregano
3. Mum
4. English ivy
5. Fernspray false cypress
6. Autumn fern
7. Ornamental grass

ACCENT AN
Outdoor Fireplace

Use seasonal color or soft evergreens to add oomph to your outdoor fireplace. Regardless of the sason, a grouping of pots will help bring warmth and welcome anytime of year.

◄ PLAN FOR THE YEAR

When a fireplace is a focal point of your outdoor space, plant pots that look great almost year-round. The lush asparagus fern and false cypress provide virtually year-round green accents. The mums tucked into the centerpiece and featured in each of the anchor pots bring a lively touch of color and can be changed with the seasons.

KEEP A CONSTANT

Ferns, cypress, and succulents add texture and soft color to any brick, stone, or painted fireplace. Using a variety of only green plants allows the textures to stand out, adding visual interest to your outdoor room without overwhelming it with color. Remember to keep one constant. Here, the pots are similar colors, shapes, or both.

CREATE
Focal Points

While pretty pots are a classic way to flank your entryway, container gardening doesn't stop there. Frequently containers are used as a focal point—a device in garden design that gives visitors a place to rest their gaze.

SCALE IT RIGHT ▶

An ideal focal point would be a pot large enough to be in scale with its setting and capture attention, even at a distance. That distance could be across a 10-foot lawn in a townhome garden or at the end of a vista 50 or 100 feet away.

STAND OUT

It also helps to create a frame around the focal point, a path leading to it, or a background that makes it stand out from the surroundings. A hedge offers an even texture behind a bold one. A background of lawn or sky will make contrasting colors stand out. Once the focal point is noticed, it should be interesting enough to warrant further attention. Then there should be sufficient detail in the planting or the area around it to not disappoint when the visitor views it up close.

USE REPETITION TO YOUR ADVANTAGE

The repetition of three large pots here brings drama and privacy. Hollies offer a screen with the benefit of berries in the winter. The taller choices of hollies range from Savannah (35 feet), Mary Nell (25 to 30 feet), Burford (20 feet), and Willowleaf (15 feet).

Screening
FOR PRIVACY

With small properties and tightly set homes, screening offers the benefits of privacy on both sides of the property line. Restricted root zones compromise any effort to plant a green screen, and every homeowner's desire for privacy makes quick growth imperative. Containers are the answer, both for the plants and the gardener.

CHOOSE THE RIGHT CONTAINER ▶

Container-grown bamboo, as well as upright conifers and broad-leaved evergreens, offer fast-growing visual boundaries where only the property line existed before. Horse troughs are sturdy, long, and narrow, and they come with a drain. Consider these when a quick screen is needed.

ROOM FOR THE ROOTS

Keep in mind that for plants to grow tall, they need to have room for their roots to anchor them against blowing over and to support them with nutrition and moisture. Big pots are needed for big plants.

A MORE
Graphic Garden

If a gardener seeks a groomed and formal design or has an abundant menagerie of flowering plants that lacks a cohesive design, the solution in either case is to create order in the outdoor plantings. Thoughtfully placed pots holding rigid, geometric forms become sentinels of order and contrast.

FANCY PLANTS ▶

Make a playful yet effective choice for creating order in the garden. Plants pruned to be a ball on a stick are called "standards." The style is the result of a horticultural practice called topiary. Most often you will see multiple orbs of greenery that appear to be stacked on a stem or foliage clipped into spirals that appear to twist around the stem. The plants grown in these clipped forms vary widely and may include (but are not limited to) roses, rosemary, lantana, ligustrum, conifers, and the green tower options listed below.

A FEW GREEN TOWERS

- *Buxus sempervirens* 'Dee Runk'
- *Chamaecyparis pisifera* 'Baby Blue'
- *Ilex crenata* 'Sky Pencil'
- *Ilex vomitoria* 'Will Fleming'
- *Picea glauca* 'Haal'
- *Podocarpus macrophylla* 'Maki'
- *Thuja occidentalis* 'Degroot's Spire'

CREATING ORDER ▲

The quickest, most effective, and most affordable means of creating order out of chaos in your garden is to make use of structural plants in pots. A green orb, cone, or spire, chosen with good proportion to a pot, can help punctuate the design. Positioned to frame an entrance, mark corners, or even create a focal point, these plants-in-pots are hardworking and rewarding additions.

The plants most commonly used to make these graphic orbs are boxwoods, conifers, or hollies. Likewise, a tall slender boxwood, conifer, or holly may also be the best choice to add some visual height in your garden space. (These would of course be different selections from those chosen for orbs.) Each will grow naturally into the desired form (see page 25). They are not necessarily dependent upon pruning, although sometimes pruning helps to realize the goal.

A FEW GREEN ORBS

- *Buxus sempervirens* 'Suffruticosa'
- *Buxus* x 'Baby Gem', 'Glencoe', 'Green Gem', 'Green Velvet'
- *Buxus sinica* var. *insularis* 'Justin Brouwers'
- *Chamaecyparis pisifera* 'Filifera Aurea'
- *Cryptomeria japonica* 'Globosa Nana'
- *Thuja occidentalis* 'Hetz Midget', 'Rheingold'

GO
Bold

Some container gardens are created for a soothing effect in the swelter of summer, but it's also fun to do the opposite—embrace the hot season with bold colors and patterns that energize and excite.

CONTAINER RECIPE

1. SunPatiens™ Orange
2. Alternanthera
3. Coleus 'Tigerlily'
4. Melampodium 'Million Gold'
5. Golden creeping Jenny

◀ BALANCING ACT

The hot summer colors used in this container look even more vivid when balanced with the cool green of Southern shield fern and creeping Jenny. The accent of lime green also makes the vibrant colors stand out even more.

CATCH FIRE ▼

The vast variety of eye-catching coleus is one way to amp up the color in your containers. Here, a trio of pots flaunts their intense flame-like foliage against cool blue hydrangeas. It's a contrast that's a reflection of the summer season.

'Dipt in Wine'

'Alligator Tears'

'Trailing Red'

CHOOSE YOUR HUE
From red to green to purple, these
coleus varieties top our list for fantastic
color and performance.

'Beckswith's Gem'

'Indian Summer'

'Henna'

PARE DOWN THE
Palette

A more monochromatic color palette can be a soothing visual relief, a place for your eyes to rest.

▼ GO FOR A WHITE OUT

Transitional spaces, like the side yard shown here, blossom into a feature of your home with a focused color scheme and thoughtfully chosen plants. The all-white palette with a relaxed style is a beautiful contrast to the more structured green lawn.

CONTAINER RECIPE

1. 'Surfinia White Improved' petunias

DAZZLING WHITES
As a contrast to brightly hued plants, try these hardworking annuals, perennials, and shrubs.

Lily-of-the-valley

Asiatic lily

'David' summer phlox

Dusty miller

'White Out' shrub rose

Lamb's ears

Spotted dead nettle

Shasta daisy

'Icicle' Veronica

CONTAINER RECIPE

1. 'Aaron' white caladium
2. 'Key Lime Pie' heuchera
3. Holly fern
4. 'White Nancy' spotted dead nettle
5. English ivy
6. Light pink periwinkle

ADD CHARM WITH
Window Boxes

If you lack the time, money, or energy to maintain a large garden or simply lack the space, window boxes provide an opportunity to enjoy colorful flowers and foliage in smaller doses.

◄ PROVIDE CONSISTENT CARE

Window boxes need regular attention. Start with quality potting mix that contains lots of organic matter, stays moist, and drains well (see page 18). Remove spent flowers promptly to encourage more flowers. Fertilize twice a month using a liquid blossom-boosting product.

SCALE IT RIGHT ▶

A proper window box should be the same width or extend beyond the window by a few inches.

CHOOSE THE BEST PLANTS ▶

Mix trailing plants that cascade over the sides with tall plants in the center of the box and mounding plants on the sides. Don't plant something that grows too tall and hides your window, unless privacy is your main objective.

Succession
PLANTING

Give containers of hardy evergreens some seasonal appeal by rotating colorful plants in and out. Changing just one plant is also more cost effective.

STAPLE PLANTS

Front door containers can have structural plants that stay constant and look great throughout the year. If pots are close to the door, stairs, or walk, avoid plants with leaves that are thorny or have sharp edges such as spiny hollies, mahonia, barberry, and yucca. Here are a few of our top choices:

- Boxwood
- Autumn fern
- Sasanqua camellia
- cast-iron plant
- Palm
- Clipped ligustrum
- Needle palm
- Algerian ivy

WHEN IT'S TIME TO CHANGE THE BASE

When the base plant in a pot is healthy and the roots have not yet filled the potting mix, you can let it remain as a year-round anchor plant. (You can also have multiple base plants in a container, if you like.) However, once the roots fill the potting mix, they begin competing for light, water, and nutrients, making it difficult to plant seasonal color around the edges. You'll know when it happens because the performance of the annuals will decline. You can either maintain the pots without seasonal color, or pull all the plants out and try a new combination. Whether you just replant the color or change the whole pot, it's a fun project that takes a few hours at the most, and it is almost like you have re-landscaped.

ADDING SEASONAL PLANTS

Once you have your base plants set, all that's needed is to add some color. This is the component that will change seasonally to be sure there are always flowers at the front door. An example: Pentas plants have long-lasting summer flowers and butterflies love them. Then in the fall when the cool season annuals appear in the garden center, substitute your favorite color of pansies for the pentas. Consider a trailing type such as Cool Wave or WonderFall pansies. These will endure all but the coldest of winters, blooming nicely in fall, throughout a mild winter, and abundantly in spring.

SMALL-SPACE
Container Gardens

For gardeners who have small courtyards or patios, balconies,
rooftop gardens, or just have limited outdoor space,
containers can create an aesthetically pleasing garden.
You can plant anywhere there is room for a pot.

SOFTEN A STAIRCASE ▶

Using a series of potted plants, one for each step, creates a beautiful edge to stairways. When the containers and plants are the same, the results are harmonious and uniform, but a mix of plants and pots can add interest and color. Here, boxwood topiaries turn an otherwise blank spot into a pretty vignette and add a touch of formality.

MAKE THE MOST OF EVERY SQUARE INCH ▶

Areas underneath stairs may have gone unused or been overlooked, but this is prime real estate for potted plants. Bring interest with a surprising burst of green. Here, ferns and variegated ivy surround an urn filled with colorful caladiums.

◀ ADORN A TABLETOP

Using containers on your outdoor tabletop is another way to add life to your space, no matter the size. Here, a dwarf arborvitae topiary and low-growing creeping vine won't drop leaves into your morning coffee.

CONTAINER RECIPE

1. 'Flapjacks' kalanchoe
2. 'Coppertone' sedum
3. 'Perle von Nurnberg' echeveria
4. 'Blue' senecio
5. 'Red Stem' portulacaria
6. 'Zorro' echeveria
7. 'Black Knight' echeveria
8. 'Violet Queen' echeveria

Succulents

You won't find any plants better adapted for growing in pots than succulents. Mostly native to arid regions, succulents store water in their thick, waxy leaves, stems, and roots, enabling them to resist drought, which means they don't need to be fussed over with frequent watering.

◄ POTTING BASICS

One thing these low-maintenance plants require is excellent drainage. If the roots sit in water or mucky soil, they quickly rot. To ensure proper drainage, buy a potting mix for succulents or make your own. Use a traditional potting mix and blend it with an equal part of crushed granite, expanded shale, poultry grit, or pumice sold in bags for use in animal stalls. This will make the potting mix drain faster and dry more quickly—just the conditions that succulents need. Avoid using plastic pots that trap moisture. Clay, concrete, and stone are better.

PLANTING ►

Succulents don't need lots of space. Although some mature to the size of a shrub or small tree, most grow slowly to less than 2 feet tall and put up with crowded roots. This allows you to grow them in shallow pots and mix three or four types together. One of the great attractions of succulents is how the different textures, colors, forms, and foliage combine in a single pot. Just remember, the more sun they get, the better off they will be—not just during the winter, but in the transition back outdoors in spring.

WATERING SUCCULENTS

Water thoroughly once a week so that water flows out of the drainage hole. Let the soil go dry between waterings. In winter, water only once a month.

FERTILIZER

Feed every two to three weeks with a general purpose liquid fertilizer diluted to half strength. In winter, stop fertilizing.

HOW TO PLANT SUCCULENTS

1. Fill a wide, shallow dish three-quarters full with potting mix for succulents (see page 85); cover the top with gravel.
2. Blend thoroughly, and then moisten with water.
3. Remove the plants from their nursery containers, and plant the largest one on one side of the pot. Surround it with the other plants, clustering similar shapes together.
4. Sprinkle mulch, such as gravel or pebbles, around each plant so the soil is covered. This reduces the humidity around the plants and gives the surface of the container a finished appearance.

Succulents may or may not live through winter, depending on where you live. When winter is near, you can shelter the pot of tender succulents, bringing it into your home, greenhouse, or heated garage. If you don't want to bother with them, you can let them go or gift them to someone who has shelter for them. However, if starting over each spring does not appeal to you, grow those that will withstand freezes. Many are low and spreading sedums such as *Sedum album*, *S. acre*, *S. corsicum*, *S. kamtschaticum*, *S. lineare* 'Variegatum', *S. makinoi*, *S. reflexum*, *S. spurium*, and many more. Known affectionately as hen and chicks, the various forms of *Sempervivum* endure the cold, as do some ice plants (*Delosperma* sp.). Gardeners in USDA Zone 7 and warmer can enjoy ghost plant (*Graptopetalum paraguayense*) for its remarkable tolerance to single-digit temperatures. For all of these, good drainage is essential for them to survive the winter.

Sempervivum arachnoideum: winter hardy; tightly packed, pointed leaves look like little artichokes; grows 4 inches high; reddish summer blossoms; often called cobweb

Sedum spathulifolium: winter hardy; small, spoon-shaped, blue-green leaves on trailing stems; grows 4 inches tall and 12 inches wide; light yellow flowers in summer

Echeveria 'Silver Onion': hardy to 25 degrees; forms cabbage-like clusters of silvery leaves 6 inches tall and 8 inches wide, often called hen and chicks

A SUCCULENT SAMPLER

There's an endless array of succulent forms available and many garden centers carry a wide variety. Mix and match upright ones with trailing ones for an eclectic look, or pick your favorite and showcase it in a container.

Aloe vera: tender to frost; grows up to 2 feet tall; stiff, upright leaves with cream stripes; sap used to treat burns and bites; spikes of yellow flowers in spring or summer

Sedum makinoi 'Limelight': winter hardy; whorls of small, chartreuse leaves; trailing, mat-forming habit; grows 2 inches tall and 12 inches wide; likes partial shade

Kalanchoe thyrsiflora 'Flapjack': tender to frost; paddle-shaped, gray-green leaves turn red in full sun; grows 8 inches tall and wide

Kalanchoe pumila 'Silver Gray': tender to frost; silvery green leaves; trailing; grows 3 to 6 inches tall; showy, pink flowers in winter; likes cool temperatures indoors

Sedum rupestre 'Blue Spruce': winter hardy; blue-green, needle-like foliage; forms a mat; grows 4 to 6 inches tall and 24 inches wide; bright yellow

BULB
Pots

So often we think of reworking pots for summer, tweaking them for fall, and then either emptying them or planting winter-hardy material for spring. Yet for all the attention to pansies, sweet Williams, wallflowers, calendula, and other spring flowers, bulbs are frequently overlooked. They shouldn't be. Most are perfectly winter hardy in areas with hard freezes, even in pots. Best of all, they warm up before the bulbs in the ground do, so they bloom earlier and signal the onset of spring.

WHAT BULBS TO PLANT ▲

In gardens in the Lower South (USDA Zone 8) where bulbs do not get sufficient cold to bloom normally, they have their best chance above ground in pots, exposed to the chill. Gardeners in those regions should select bulbs that are specified to bloom early. That means they need the least amount of cold weather to break their dormancy and flower. By all means, buy them pre-chilled if possible to hedge your bets. If you live in an area that does not get below 40 degrees Fahrenheit, you shouldn't try to grow the spring flowering bulbs such as tulips, hyacinths, crocus, and daffodils. But don't feel deprived. You have bulbs such as amaryllis and paperwhite narcissus that need no chilling, not to mention tropical bulbs, summer bulbs, and flowering plants.

PLANTING BULBS

1. When planting bulbs in a pot, think of them like the filling between layers of a cake. Put in some potting mix, place the larger bulbs close together in the deepest layer, but not so close that they touch.
2. Add more potting mix on top of the bulbs. If there are smaller bulbs you can make another layer, or just plant your winter annuals on the top. The bulbs will push through the annuals when the time is right, blooming above them.

WINTER
Pots

The South is blessed with mild winters in most of the region, so Southerners garden year-round, even in pots. While the materials vary greatly, depending on the severity of the winter, gardeners are ever resourceful.

WHAT REGIONS WORK FOR WINTER POTS

In the coldest regions of the country, most containers are not hardy enough. If the hardware fails, there is no reason to plant. Most containers are emptied and put away for the season. However, in the Middle, Lower, and Coastal South (USDA hardiness Zones 7–10) containers get a new planting scheme and the show continues.

◀ COLD-HARDY PLANTS

Conifers are go-to evergreens. They are cold hardy and are usually spherical or conical. This firm contrast of green to the random bare branches of the winter landscape is a welcome sight. They create order.

Other cold-hardy plants include the winter greens—these are as loose as the conifers are rigid. While not all are reliably hardy, kale is among the toughest, followed by collards. These, as well as Swiss chard and mustard, create height in containers that would otherwise be a flat flowering of pansies, violas, dianthus, lobelia, sweet alyssum, and such.

Deciduous shrubs such as forsythia, flowering almond, daphne, kerria, quince, and paper bush are leafless like many of the plants in the garden, but as spring begins, they offer their early blossoms as a harbinger of the flowers to come. Set in pots that have early spring bulbs in addition to a topping of winter annuals, and the season will unfurl at your door. Many are fragrant, and their sweetness will cut through the lingering chill to delight all who pass by, reminding them that spring is just around the corner.

CONTAINER RECIPE

1. Monterey cypress
2. Possumhaw branches
3. Variegated English ivy
4. 'White Peacock' ornamental kale
5. White cyclamen
6. 'Blush Pink' Nandina

A WELCOMING BALANCE

The combination of soothing green (ferns) and colorful annuals (like impatiens) gives an inviting feel to this entry. Bold, bright annuals are a welcome sign of the season at this front doorway. Not to mention, a beautiful view from inside the home.

Vertical Gardening

Elevate
THE APPEAL

Take your plants to new heights and give your garden an added layer of interest. Elevated containers raise your gaze so you can view beautiful plants at arm's length, eye level, or even higher.

◄ NOT TOO HIGH!

Hanging baskets offer an easy way to raise the level of flowers and greenery around your home. It's tempting to just hang the plant in its plastic pot on a hook under your eave or the roof of your porch; but if the container is above your head, you'll see as much of the bottom of the pot as the plant that's in it. To fully appreciate the beauty of the hanging plant, consider lowering the hanging basket with an S-hook, chain, shepherd's hook, or bracket so you can enjoy more than just the tips of the trailing stems.

Another consideration is the plastic pot itself, which may not always be an aesthetic asset. It's easy to repot the plant from a hanging basket into a more suitable wire basket with a coir liner. When repotting, choose a larger basket to give your plants more of everything they need to grow (see page 16).

HANG IN GROUPS ▶

Sturdy tree limbs, arbors, gazebos, and even porch eaves provide ideal spots for hanging plants in groups. Apply the same guidelines you would use for groups of pots on the ground (see page 34). Make the containers different heights by hooking them to lengths of chain or S-hooks to extend their drop. Think of the grouping of baskets as you would a garden, taking care to repeat or contrast colors, textures, and plant forms.

BRIDGE THE DIVIDE ▼

Create a harmonious transition between house and garden with green and blooming plants that tumble from hanging baskets, sit prettily atop walls, or spill over deck railings. As with all containers, such adaptable positioning enables plants to beautify places where they otherwise could not grow, while adding a welcoming elegance to the places we live. See page 96 for more about vertical gardening.

CHOOSING CONTAINERS FOR
Vertical Gardening

Like all forms of container gardening, successful vertical gardening begins with choosing the right containers. While baskets and hayracks with coated wire frames and coir liners are common, there are many other inspiring choices available. As always, consider price, style, compatibility, and durability when you shop.

BASKETS ▶

A wicker basket woven on a wire frame has an elegant, handcrafted style that complements anything planted in it. Lined with a perforated plastic sheet, the basket is slow to degrade and lasts several years before the wicker breaks down. The chain or wire should be sturdy enough to hold the weight of a planted and watered basket. Here, a hefty chain gives good support and the appearance of strength, enhancing the look of a well-made, nicely planted container.

An idea: Try hanging a finial from the point of the container. An old chandelier crystal is ideal because it will add a flash of sparkle to the pot and will tolerate water draining over it daily.

CONTAINER RECIPE

Muted gray-greens tie this planting together.
1. Echeveria
2. Oyster plant
3. String of pearls
4. Rush

ORBS

Spherical forms offer the option of planting a minimalist basket. The metal form provides the overall shape, regardless of your plant choices. It creates the illusion of a terrarium but without the glass. Within the overarching wire, the plants form a beautiful arrangement.

DECK JOCKEYS ▶

Containers designed to ride a deck railing are available in resin and wood, as well as coated wire and coir-lined models. When lushly planted, these convey the feeling of being in a garden surrounded by flowers when you are simply sitting on your deck. Also available are brackets that enable you to hang terra-cotta or resin pots from a railing or a wall. However, these may not work as well as the larger rectangular containers that hold more soil, since small pots—especially terra-cotta—dry out quickly on a hot, sunny deck.

◀ RUSTIC CONTAINERS

Galvanized buckets and tubs can be used to make charmingly simple hanging containers. These will need drainage holes as well as holes in the rim for a rope or S-hooks and a chain. Versatile galvanized containers are well suited to a variety of garden looks, from casual country to urban industrial style.

Consider an old pulley as a clever way to hang a container that goes beyond the standard hook or eyebolt. And if the pulley isn't too rusted, you may be able to use it in a practical way—to lower and raise the planting for maintenance.

When it comes to rustic containers, nothing is better than a vintage colander, minnow bucket, bicycle basket, little red wagon, child's peddle car or truck, or other such relics of bygone times that will hold soil and drain. Flea markets are a good source for such imaginative planters that will add charm and whimsy to the garden. So head to the flea market and don't forget to take your imagination.

COMBINATION
Baskets

Not all baskets need to be only one kind and color of plant. Planting a combination of plants in a large wire frame with a coir liner will make a colorful, professional-looking basket.

SELECTING THE PLANT COMBINATION

When choosing your mix of plants, keep in mind their ultimate form and size. You can apply the thriller, filler, and spiller rule of thumb for containers (see page 20) but with some variation. The *thriller* does not need to be too tall because the depth of soil in the basket cannot support it. In general, look for a plant with a height 1½ to 2 times the depth of the basket. Even in big baskets, go with a moderate-size thriller such as a large caladium, 'Festival Burgundy' cordyline, or a small ornamental grass such as 'Fireworks' or 'Sky Rocket' pennisetum.

If your *filler* will grow tall enough, skip the thriller and opt for 'Diamond Frost' euphorbia, compact or spreading SunPatiens, pentas, vinca, or angelonia in the sun. In the shade, select a shade-loving dwarf caladium, impatiens, coleus, crossandra, or a small tropical foliage plant such as 'Limelight' or 'Lemon Lime' dracaena, angel-wing begonia, or 'Prince of Orange' philodendron.

There are many choices of *spillers*, including trailing verbena, calibrachoa, petunia, sweet alyssum, portulaca, pothos, creeping Jenny, lantana, torenia, asparagus fern, and dwarf English ivy.

MAKE IT GREAT

With a little thought for the design of the basket in the setting where it will hang, a nice basket becomes a great basket. It just requires a little observation. Think about the colors in the area around your basket—in the walls of your home, in the outdoor furniture, and in the other plants that will be in the vicinity of the basket. If you have orange-red brick, select flowers and foliage that are compatible. If there are blue cushions on your chairs, use blue flowers in your basket.

Assess the scale of the area where the basket will hang. If it is large, a small basket may get lost. In this case, consider planting one large basket or grouping several baskets (see page 95) at different heights in different sizes to fill the space.

PLANTING A BASKET WITH A COIR LINER

1. Place the wire frame on a stable surface that is a comfortable height for planting. If the bottom of the frame is rounded or comes to a point, use an empty pot beneath it to cradle it and keep it steady while you work.

2. Put the coir liner in place. Because water can drain out of the liner so easily, you will want to slow its progress so the potting mix will have time to absorb it. Do this by cutting pieces of plastic from the potting mix bag or a trash can liner. You don't want to totally cover the inside surface of the coir, but you want to create a shallow bowl in the lowest portion, a bowl with small holes in it.

3. After you have the plastic liner in place, scoop the potting mix into the liner. Add slow-release granular fertilizer at the rate recommended on the label.

4. Water gently with a breaker nozzle (see page 46), and then reposition the coir liner as the soil settles to support it from the inside.

5. Gather your plants. Once you set your plants in place, you'll need to water again.

6. Once the basket is planted, fill any sunken areas with potting mix. Water well one last time. If the basket is large and heavy, you may want to get help to lift and hang it before the final watering.

◄ ON A PEDESTAL

Pots on posts are a popular hardware purchase for those who enjoy growing in containers. This type of planter comes in a kit that includes a metal frame with a coir liner along with a post which can be installed in a garden bed or in a pot on a hard surface. The latter forms a floral topiary with two tiers of color.

DRESS UP WALLS ►

Containers become living finials when used on top of masonry walls, especially where there is a column. If the wall is low, or you would like an additional sense of separation, a rectangular planter with tall, wispy grasses or salvia may be just the answer. If you are looking for a more formal greeting as guests step through an opening in a wall, potted boxwoods are like verdant sentinels at the gate. For a sense of carefree elegance, place urns overflowing with flowers atop columns.

◀ RISE ABOVE

Tall urns and pots on pedestals or plinths help containers rise to the scale of the garden around them. If your garden is less formal, turn a pot of equal size upside down and use it as a pedestal for the planted one on top, base to base. Then group other, shorter ones around it.

Raise
THEM UP

Hanging a basket of container-grown plants is an easy way to raise the level of interest in the garden, but you can also support containers and their plants in other engaging ways.

ADD HEIGHT TO CONTAINERS ▶

Tame climbers such as a large-flowered clematis can be used on a tuteur, or conical trellis, to raise the color and give the planting increased height. Anchored inside the pot, a tuteur is usually underplanted with a trailing plant to give fullness at the base.

CONTAINER RECIPE

1. 'H. F. Young' clematis
2. 'Diamond Frost' euphorbia
3. Purple torenia
4. Variegated ivy

CREATE A
Living Wall

Frames that hold soil and attach to the wall offer an ideal way to add plantings in a space too confined for potted plants. These frames can be a planter and trellis combined, or plantable rectangles or circles (wreaths). They are especially useful for gardeners with too little space to plant.

GREEN RELIEF ▼

Many outdoor walls are just blank canvases that can be handily transformed into lush living walls. A wall planting system is inexpensive and easy to plant, hang, and maintain. The basic unit (kinsmangarden.com) consists of a frame measuring 14 inches tall and wide by 5 inches deep. It's lined with a coco-fiber mat with planting holes cut into the sides and front. You can hang two units together to make a rectangle or four units to make a large square. Plant starting at the bottom and adding soil and plants as you go. Begin with the bottom row by adding some potting mix, soaking the root balls of the transplants in water, then pushing the roots through the holes. Add more potting mix and plants to the rows above to fill out the wall. When combining two or more units, don't plant the adjoining edges or you'll squash the leaves in between.

HOW TO HANG A LIVING WALL

Each planting unit is hung from the wall by two metal J-hooks. The hooks allow air between the top of the planting unit and the wall to prevent moisture damage. Insert spacers, such as plastic bottle caps, at each bottom corner if you're hanging the unit on wooden siding. Be sure to clear the area just below your living arrangement of anything that may be damaged by the occasional stray drop of water.

◀ WHAT TO PLANT IN A LIVING WALL

Annual flowers such as 'Dragon Wing' begonia, coleus, gomphrena, lantana, and sweet potato vine are good planting options for living walls. Foliage plants such as pothos, spider plant, fern, ivy, arrowhead vine, and dracaena, as well as succulents, are also good choices.

HOW TO WATER A LIVING WALL

Gently water the living wall by hand from the top, allowing the water to reach all the way to the bottom. It's time to water when the plants wilt or the soil feels dry.

CONTAINER RECIPE

1. Ivy
2. Nerve plant
3. Spider plant
4. Pink arrowhead vine
5. Variegated dracaena
6. 'Neon' pothos
7. Fern

Growing Up

Paved courtyards, common in both historic and modern townhomes, as well as off-ground decks, present a challenge for gardeners. Inevitably, there is blank paving and a blank wall without soil to support planting. Container-grown plants with structural support are a practical solution to covering these bare surfaces with flowers and greenery.

FINDING THE RIGHT SUPPORT ▶

Frames for a trellis or espalier can be crafted to suit the setting by a carpenter or metalsmith, or you can purchase prefab designs from home and garden supply companies. Commonly, frames are made in grid or fan shapes. Hardware, such as long-shanked, threaded hooks, is used to hold the frame on a wooden or masonry surface. Set the container below the frame, and plant.

The long shank on the hook holds the frame and growing vine away from the wall. This has two advantages. The first is to allow air circulation and avoid moisture or mold problems on the wall. The second is to allow the vine to twine around the support or to give the gardener space to attach a non-twining vine or shrub to the frame.

◀ SUPPORT YOUR PLANTS

Supports such as fanciful tuteurs (see page 101) or even a basic structure of stakes and string can transform a flowering vine into a colorful garden feature. Anchored in the potting soil, the structure, resembling a small tepee, grows more sturdy as the vine takes hold and weighs it down. The vine may need some guidance to remain within the structure, rather than reaching out and grasping a nearby shrub or tree Use multiples of these supports to define an area, to separate adjacent areas, or add some height to an area. Used against a wall, they offer a welcome interruption of the blank expanse. On a deck or rooftop garden, they can give a sense of enclosure and separation from the world beyond.

A plant trained into a two-dimensional pattern is called an espalier. The difference between a plant on a trellis and a plant that has been espaliered is that the espalier is tightly trained and conforms to a rigid pattern. Usually it is a shrub or tree with branches that will grow thick with age.

You can make a two-dimensional support for a trellis or espalier that stands in a pot or attaches to a nearby wall. Usually made of metal or wood, the frame is raised from the surface of the wall so that plants can attach to it. Use a large container, and guide the plant onto the frame. In small gardens or areas without room to plant, this technique provides the subtle softness and cooling of a green wall without taking up precious space.

Take Care

Use the best practices of container gardening (planting, watering, and fertilizing), as explained in Chapter 1. Train vines or shrubs onto a trellis or espalier frame by attaching and pruning.

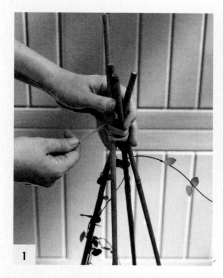

HOW TO MAKE YOUR OWN TUTEUR

You can make your own tuteur from bamboo and twine.
1. Stick the bamboo into the potting soil, angling the sticks toward the center of the pot.
2. Lash them together with jute twine for a natural look. Tip: Don't trim away all of the little branches on the bamboo. They are helpful in training a vine.

PROPER PRUNING

Pruning branch tips forces the plant to grow side branches. Sometimes you will need to remove extra or errant branches. During the growing season, any plant trained into a rigid espalier pattern needs almost weekly attention to be sure that the design is accomplished and maintained.

CREATE A TRELLIS

If having a frame is not as important to you as the pattern of the plant, make your own trellis by using wood or masonry screws and galvanized wire. Create a pattern on the adjacent wall or fence by anchoring the screws near and far, and stretch the wire between them. Then train the plant to follow the lines made by the wire. The wire will largely disappear, so the plant takes center stage.

ATTACHING THE PLANTS

Attach the plant using soft ties such as hook-and-loop tape or twine. Many vines such as Carolina jessamine, coral honeysuckle, and mandevilla will twine, while others such as English ivy, climbing hydrangea, Boston ivy, and fig vine will attach themselves without structure, if you don't mind them adhering to your wall. No matter how your plant grows, you will readily see a way to guide it in the direction you want it to grow just by observing. The key is training it little by little over time.

On the other hand, you can use a less-structured method. Try growing a tropical, annual, or a small perennial vine, and let it scamper about on its trellis or deck railing. You will have a soft, green surface with a lot less work. Loosely guide the plant onto the trellis without much thought to the pattern. The support supplies the pattern, and the plant drapes on it or twines around it.

Vines suited to life in a container are large-flowered clematis, fatshedera, and cherry tomatoes, to name a few. Shrubs that can be grown in a container and trained to a frame include roses ('Cécile Brünner', 'Ducher', 'Else Poulsen', 'Marie Daly', 'Perle d'Or', or 'The Fairy'), sweet kumquats, and dwarf sasanqua camellias.

GO UP

For limited floor space, a tuteur may be the perfect solution. Adding containers with tall visual interest gives a small space a bigger feel. These two containers draw your eye up and out while also framing the space.

CONSIDER SHAPE AND SIZE

Adding a mix of large and small pots and using plants that have variation in the shape of their leaves brings interest and warmth to a room. Think of places to add tall plants and consider medium to small plants for end tables and smaller spaces.

Indoor Containers

POTTED PLANTS
Indoors

Those who love plants naturally want to bring them into their homes. Plants offer a softening effect and make a house feel like a sanctuary.

WHY HOUSEPLANTS?

Having plants in your home means there is a lot of give-and-take going on—they take care of us as much as we take care of them. Plants clean the air of our closed, indoor environments, making our homes healthier, both in a physical and psychological sense. Having plants indoors brings the subliminal comfort of nature into our climate-controlled rooms. Flowering houseplants, foliage plants, and indoor trees all make growing container plants indoors a pleasure.

FLOWER POWER ▶

Flowering houseplants are as decorative as cut flowers. They bring the same luxuriousness to the dining table, end table, or bedside with minimal expense or effort—no arranging required. With a little care, most blooms will last for weeks and some even longer.

Not all of the flowering plants you see in stores are actually houseplants. Some are gift plants, intended to be enjoyed and discarded. Spring flowering bulbs such as a pot of narcissus or hyacinths are grown in pots for the gift plant market, as are azalea, calla lily, hydrangea, chrysanthemum, gloxinia, kalanchoe, poinsettia, and others. Sometimes they make the transition into a garden, and sometimes not.

Others such as African violet, anthurium, Christmas cactus, clivia, moth orchid, crossandra, and peace lily are suited to taking up residence in your home, especially if you live where winter will kill a tropical plant. These will bloom again and again if you care for them.

INDOOR PLANT
Arrangements

Plants bring life and add interest to your home. Here are a few tips for incorporating them effectively.

MIXED POTS INDOORS

To elevate your indoor plants beyond the one-plant-in-one-pot paradigm, try combining several plants for a captivating display. Applying all the principles of contrasting plant size, form, color, and texture used for outdoor containers, you can assemble arrangements in indoor pots that last far longer than cut flowers.

A planter of mixed foliage plants will coexist happily for months, if not years, depending on the plants you choose, their care, and growing conditions. Plant them all together in potting mix, or maintain them in separate pots, using a larger container as a cachepot. Remember, combination pots are only successful if the plants in the pot need similar light and growing conditions. If one likes it wet and one dry, the arrangement will inevitably fail.

Flame violet

FLOWERS & FOLIAGE

Some plants produce foliage that's so attractive you would have grown them just for their leaves. The flowers are the icing on the cake.

Walking iris

- FLAME VIOLET (*Episcia cupreata*) comes in an assortment of flower colors and silvery leaf patterns. It likes bright, indirect light and warmth, just like its African violet cousins.

- WALKING IRIS (*Neomarica caerulea*) looks like an iris that has pups like a spider plant. It will be happy by any window, blooming in late winter and spring. The 2-inch flowers open in the morning and close by night.

- JEWEL ORCHID (*Ludisia discolor*) has leaves of brown velvet striped with red. Spikes of white flower clusters appear at the ends of the stems.

Jewel orchid

- EUCHARIST LILY (*Eucharis amazonica*) is a handsome green-leaved bulb that blooms in spring. The flower is clear white, 2 to 3 inches across, and deliciously fragrant.

- WAX FLOWER (*Hoya carnosa*) is a low-maintenance, drought-tolerant addition to the home, ideal for a hanging basket or plant stand. It likes bright light. Flowers are waxy pendant clusters, sweetly perfumed.

- FIRE LILY (*Clivia miniata*) is a handsome bulb that quietly grows dark green for most of the year. After cooler temperatures in the winter (not freezing), it will bloom in a spherical cluster of orange flowers, each one with a yellow throat.

Eucharist lily

Wax flower

Fire lily

PLANTS WITH STATURE

Indoor trees can make even a big, impersonal room with a vaulted ceiling seem intimate and warm by creating an enclosure. Place trees next to or between furniture to help define a sitting area in a large room, or use them to create a passageway or a spot to linger. For plants that function as a part of your home's design, not huddled next to the windows, be sure to buy ones that are appropriately sized for the space.

▲ MANAGING EXPECTATIONS

No matter what time of day, interiors simply don't have the intensity of light that plants need to really grow. It's unlikely that plants challenged by minimal light will have growth spurts, and moving them outdoors for summer and back indoors for winter usually creates problems with sunburned leaves outside and dropping leaves inside. Adjust your care to the plant's needs.

Avoid pushing your plants with water and fertilizer. Be content with a plant that is green and pretty, without much increase in size. For moderate light situations, the best choices are 'Alii' ficus, fiddleleaf fig, corn plant, lady palm, and rubber plant. All of these will benefit from even more light, if possible. If you have bright indoor light, try growing ponytail palm, schefflera, or giant yucca.

CREATE A PLANT POCKET

Nothing enhances a short-term flowering plant like surrounding it with foliage plants chosen and arranged to resemble a miniature garden. You can enjoy freshening the arrangement with a succession of flowering plants by using an empty pot as a placeholder in a mixed foliage container. Use a common size and just leave it in the planter with all the other plants rooted in the soil surrounding it. Then when you buy a fresh flowering plant, just slip the new pot inside the anchored pot for a quick change.

DECORATING WITH
Foliage

Decorators often tuck a touch of green foliage into spaces throughout homes for a fresh, organic look. When adding an accent of greenery to your room, consider these tips.

COMBINATION OF GREENS

Although a single plant can fill a space nicely, combining two or three different small plants with or without blooms brings added texture and interest.

PLACING YOUR CONTAINER

Whether it's a small 4-inch pot or a tureen, first test out the pot in the location to gauge the size plant you'll need, then fill it with appropriate foliage.

THE RIGHT HEIGHT

Picking a plant that is the right height for your space is important; different spaces will have different needs. Sometimes a room needs a plant with some vertical heft to add life to an empty corner or to cozy up an empty space next to a chair or sofa. A side table might need a smaller plant to avoid overwhelming it, while a dining table may benefit from a plant that's a little taller to create a dramatic centerpiece.

KEEP THE LIGHT IN MIND

To keep indoor plants healthy, you'll need to find a place that gets appropriate light for the plant. Side tables with lamps are prime spots, as are tables near large windows.

Tough Guys

Here are some good choices for long-term residents in your home.
While no plant will grow in the dark, these will be happy in the shadows.

◀ **LADY PALM**

(*Rhapis excelsa*) is a good indoor dweller because it grows vertically in moderate to bright light. When light is limited, the fronds, which are made up of several long fingers, seem to be bigger and more willowy, presumably to capture all the light they can. Naturally slow growing, lady palms can cost more than other houseplants, but their longevity makes them worth the price. They will be with you for years. Water regularly, and repot as needed every few years.

BROWN SPIDERWORT

(*Siderasis fuscata*) is one of the great unsung houseplants. The dark green leaves have a silvery band down the center and a cloak of reddish-purple fuzz, sort of like an African violet. However, it is much more tolerant of a busy life. Allow it to dry slightly between waterings, but if you see brown edges on the leaves, water it a little more regularly. Occasionally it will even bloom with showy purple flowers that emerge from the center of the circle of leaves. This is a good choice for a tabletop washed with gentle light from a window several feet away. There's no need to crowd the windowsill with this one.

RABBIT'S FOOT FERN ▼

(*Davallia fejeensis*) looks delicate, but it is tough enough to grow indoors. It gets its name from the furry rhizome that grows over the side of the pot. Finely divided foliage emerges along the rhizomes, making this plant ideal for hanging containers as well as tabletop ones. Keep this plant away from direct sun, and water regularly. It won't die if allowed to get a little dry. It benefits from humidity, so if you need a plant in the bathroom, this is a good choice.

PEACE LILY ▶

This plant (*Spathiphyllum* sp.) is one of the best low-light houseplants. In addition to having a range of sizes from those that reside on the end table to those that fill a corner, a peace lily has a tall, white bloom that looks like a hand raised in benediction, hence the name.

▼ POTHOS

(*Epipremnum aureum*) has been known to be happy in windowless offices that have only fluorescent lights during the day and no light all weekend. It enjoys sunlight, but only if it is indirect, filtering through a window or overhead leaves. This tropical vine can climb tall trees where it is hardy, but in a container in the home, it is happy to trail from a pot on the mantel or from the edge of a pot at the base of an indoor tree. Pothos is happy with its roots in water, but it can also be remarkably tolerant of infrequent watering. Look for selections that are green or splashed with cream or gold. Bright-green 'Neon' will brighten dark corners and contrast with other, darker plants around it.

CHINESE EVERGREEN ▶

(*Aglaonema commutatum*) is as low maintenance as a plant can be. This tabletop plant has few pests, likes to be watered when dry, and just quietly grows in the background of your life. The leaves have a mottled coloring, mostly silver on green, but some varieties, like 'Pseudobracteatum' is deep green with pale green and creamy yellow. However, this unassuming stalwart of the plant world created a lot of buzz over the past few years with brightly colored hybrids that are rimmed and splashed with red. Who needs flowers?

CAST-IRON PLANT ▼

This plant (*Aspidistra elatior*) is the poster child of low-light plants. Most Southerners know it as a garden plant, but it will live indoors as well.

CALATHEA ▶

This tabletop-sized plant (*Calathea* sp.) is happy in the ambient light of your home. It has leaves with fascinating patterns and colors displayed on dark green. Choices are many because there is such variety. It offers much and requires little.

SNAKE PLANT ▶

Also called mother-in-law's tongue, the snake plant has long suffered from its name, but more and more, gardeners refer to it by its Latin name, *Sansevieria* (san-sa-VER-e-ah). These are a diverse group of species and hybrids that can almost survive in the dark, but in indirect light they will grow long waxy leaves from underground rhizomes, eventually filling their pot. Outdoors, they will grow in bright shade to full sun during warm seasons or in frost-free areas year-round. Known to tolerate neglect, sansevierias cannot live in wet soil. Let them dry between waterings. Older pot-bound plants may even reward you for neglect with fragrant, cream-colored blooms.

1   **2**   **3**

STOCK SPLIT

When growing plants in containers, you will find your existing plants to be a great resource. If you want to add a little sansevieria (above) to a mixed pot but the plant you've had for years is too large, divide it. Here's how.

1. Carefully remove the plant from its pot. If the roots have adhered to the sides of the pot, place splayed fingers atop the soil between the leaves, turn the pot upside down, and shake gently. If that fails, tap the bottom edge of the pot gently on a hard surface. If the pot is flexible, place it on its side and press down to bend it and pop the roots free.
2. Once the plant is free of its pot, shake away loose soil and look for natural divisions. Each piece should have leaves and roots. You can use a knife or clippers to cut them apart.
3. Use a newly divided piece for each new pot, or use a piece with other species to create a mixed container. Partially fill the container with potting mix, and place the division in the pot, being careful to hold it where it will be once the potting mix can support it. Ideally, the original soil line will be the new soil line (about ½ to 1 inch below the rim of the pot). You can discern the original line where the leaves turn from white to green. Anything white would be below the new potting mix. Carefully add new mix around the roots so that they are naturally spread out in the new pot. When full, gently tap the pot on a hard surface, and then water well. Water should flow from the bottom of the pot, and the pot should feel heavy when it is thoroughly wet. If the potting mix has settled in spots, add a little more, and water again.

Semi-Tough Guys

These plants are not high maintenance in the least; however, they may require a little more attention in watering or light needs than the "Tough Guys" list.

ARROWHEAD ▶

Arrowhead (*Nephthytis* or *Syngonium*) is another low-light to medium-light grower. Keep it watered regularly, but make sure it's not too wet or soggy. With the many types of these plants in the marketplace, you may find some with a little pink, purple, or white on the leaves. Aptly named, the shape of the leaves is truly like an arrowhead, a shape that makes a lovely addition to any plant mix. Planted solo, these will fill out nicely. After a few years or a lot of fertilizer, they can become "leggy." In this case, simply trim the tall pieces and the plant will regain its fuller shape.

BIRD'S NEST FERN ▶

This plant (*Asplenium nidus*) is great for the low-light areas of your home. Watering needs are not demanding, but don't let the plant get too dry. It needs regular watering and prefers not to soak in water. Tip water from the base, not at the nest area of the plant. If you place the plant in brighter light areas, the leaves will have more of the crinkle effect. Fertilizing once a month (at most) with a liquid 20-20-20 fertilizer is sufficient.

◀ AUTUMN FERN

(*Dryopteris erythrosora*) is found in a variety of pot sizes and is a perfect addition to a group of mixed plants in a cachepot. The new growth will be an autumny coral-tinged frond. Ferns do require regular watering, but they can handle a variety of low- to bright-light situations. Most ferns like humidity, so you may want to even take this one into the bath! Seriously, it can be a great addition to a vanity. They also benefit from a little misting on the leaves, especially in the winter.

◀ ZZ PLANT

(*Zamioculcas zamiifolia*) is a very forgiving plant. If you forget to water, it's most likely going to be okay. This plant can manage through a drought. This is a slow-growing fella that will take almost any kind of light—literally from bright to low. It doesn't need much fertilizer either. We love the height it offers as well as the rich, glossy green leaves.

PROPER CARE

You need to be sensitive to what your indoor plants need. Keeping plants in light conditions below their ideal means adjusting your care regimen. They will grow more slowly and need less water and fertilizer.

▼ FIND THE RIGHT LOCATION

Container-grown houseplants are usually tropical, because the indoor environment is more consistent with the temperate climate in which tropical plants thrive. However, that doesn't mean that growing healthy houseplants is easy. While the perfect soil, moisture, and predictable temperature are easy to provide, bright light is not. You'll need to carefully pair houseplants with the available light in your home.

For many plants, an east-facing window or skylight will give them gentle morning sun that is ideal. North windows are notoriously dark. South- and west-facing windows may be too harsh for some houseplants but perfect for others. You may be surprised to see that plants on the south and west side of your home get more light in winter than in summer. That's because the leaves may have fallen from shade trees, and the sun is at a lower angle, penetrating further into the room.

CARING FOR
Indoor Plants

Indoor plants require their own type of care. Follow these tips to help your plants thrive.

▼ DUSTING AND WATERING

Without regular rainfall to wash away dust, plants will need cleaning. Dust effectively shades the leaf, and you want them to get the most light possible. The shower, preferably one with a handheld sprayer, provides the perfect place for cleaning indoor plants. Wash the leaves, spraying the top surfaces to remove dust, and then spray beneath the leaves to discourage spider mites, pests that can prosper in the low humidity of your home. On a mild day, you can take your plants outside for a hose-down in the shade. Spray the foliage, and give the potting mix a good soaking every few months. After the plants have dried and drained, move them back into place.

PROTECTING YOUR FLOORS AND FURNITURE ▼

Water is essential for houseplants, but it can be damaging to your home if it runs out of the pot. It isn't always easy to judge how much water is needed—sometimes pots that have gotten very dry won't absorb water, and it flows right through and into the saucer. (Saucers are seldom the answer anyway, since it isn't good for your plant to sit in a saucer of water long-term.)

Instead, when watering, take small plants to the kitchen sink or to the shower, especially if you see that the potting mix is dry and has shrunken away from the side of the pot. Give them a thorough watering, allowing excess water to drain. If the potting mix does not soak up the water, set the plant in a sink with about an inch of water for an hour or so.

Rather than using a saucer, you can protect your surfaces by placing your plants in a cachepot. These ceramic or metal containers have no drainage holes. Remove the plants to water them, and return them to the cachepot after they've drained.

KEEPING HOUSEPLANTS HEALTHY

Like us, houseplants can get sick from time to time. And also like us, the first line of defense against illness is to be healthy and vigorous. Here are a few things to keep in mind.

FERTILIZING: A regular program of fertilizing, once a month during the cooler months with low light and every two weeks during the growing season, is a good start. Use a soluble liquid fertilizer. Just use it instead of plain water when you are scheduled to fertilize.

DISEASES: Diseases are rare unless the soil is too wet and roots rot. For most plants, it is best to let the top inch of potting mix dry before watering again.

INSECTS: Unfortunately, insects can be a common problem. Aphids, mealybugs, and scale are the worst offenders. Indoors, pests can move from one plant to the next. Before you know it, the table or floor is sticky with the sap dripping from insects feeding. Treat infestations with horticultural oil labeled for use on indoor plants. The coating of oil suffocates insects. It is best to spray outdoors on a warm day, not colder than 50 degrees in winter or hotter than 80 degrees in summer. Let the plant dry, and bring it back indoors.

Another strategy for treating houseplants is to prune off as many infested leaves and branches as possible. Do this whether you plan to spray or not. If it is spring and you plan to take your plants outdoors to a covered porch or shaded patio, let beneficial insects such as ladybugs take care of the problem. Before bringing plants back indoors in the fall, apply a preventative oil spray to prevent a recurrence.

AVOID A SUNBURN

If your plants are burning, pull them back from the window, or use a sheer curtain to diffuse the sunlight. Never put indoor plants outside in the sun. Just like the rest of us, they will burn from sudden exposure.

Orchids

Don't let orchids intimidate you. With the right care, this plant's beautiful, delicate blooms can thrive in your home.

CARING FOR ORCHIDS

Many orchids come from the grower with sphagnum peat moss in the pot. The moss will hold moisture, so it is important to not keep the orchids too wet. You should allow them to get almost dry between waterings. Repot them when they finish blooming, removing the moss and using a mix for orchids. Place your orchid in bright shade. Generally speaking, keep the temperature between 55 and 80 degrees, and mist the orchid periodically to raise the humidity. Fertilize once or twice a month with houseplant fertilizer. Most orchids will rebloom annually and reward you for your care. To find more seasonal tips for caring for your orchids, visit **http://www.aos.org/orchids/seasonal-orchid-care.aspx.**

▼ PLANTING ORCHIDS

Although anything but rare, showy flowering orchids are, for the most part, inhabitants of the tropical tree canopy. That means they can cling to tree bark and are watered by the humid, misty air in the rain forest. When creating a pot for growing orchids, you need a potting mix labeled for orchids (traditional potting mixes are too heavy and wet). Most orchids want to grow in big chunky bark mixes that have lots of air and quick drainage. The silvery covering on their roots is adept at taking up moisture from the air and from occasional waterings. Familiar orchids that need this growing situation are moth orchids (*Phalaenopsis* sp.), oncidium orchids (*Oncidium* sp.) such as 'Sharry Baby', and tropical lady's slipper orchids (*Paphiopedilum* sp.). A cymbidium (*Cymbidium* sp.) is terrestrial, meaning it enjoys well-drained potting mix. Add a little extra bark or perlite to your bagged mix when repotting.

MOTH ORCHIDS

Moth orchids (*Phalaenopsis*) are one of the most common types available—you'll find them everywhere, from grocery stores to big-box retailers. They're fantastic plants for new gardeners because they're easy to grow and don't require a lot of attention. Plus, when combined with small ferns in a large oval cachepot, moth orchids make a dramatic impact for the dining room, entry, or any large table. Have a special event? Forego cut flowers and invest in orchids and small pot greenery for a long-lasting arrangement. Moth orchids are available in a range of sizes, colors, and blooms. Here are a few varieties.

Tying Shin Cupid 'Montclair'

Bright Peacock 'Sweet Fragrance'

Montclair 'Pink Splash'

Wenlong 'Pink Girl #1'

Yu Pin Lady 'Sogo Yukidian'

Baldan's Kaleidoscope 'Golden Treasure'

Terrariums

Low-maintenance terrariums are the perfect houseplants.
They're as easy and fun to create as they are to admire.

CONTAINER RECIPE

1. Rex begonia
2. 'White Anne' fittonia
3. Gathered mosses

CHOOSING THE CONTAINER

Choose a glass terrarium that has an opening wide enough for your hand. (You can plant in large bottles if you like using a spoon on a stick, a long funnel, and plenty of patience!) Look around your house. You may already have jars or vases that will work. Your container can have a lid, or it can be open. The more open it is, the more moisture it will require. However, this can be an advantage if you ever mistakenly overwater since there is no drainage hole for the excess moisture to drain away.

WHAT TO PLANT

Select plants that are small to allow room for growth. Good choices include moss (that you can gather or buy), succulents, miniature moth orchids, African violets, selaginella, and baby's tears. All are low growing and spreading. Plants such as peperomia, bird's nest fern, fittonia, and pteris ferns are also ideal. For ornaments, add small stones, rinsed seashells or pieces of driftwood, small ceramic figures, or even a childhood toy of sentimental significance.

PROPER CARE

Place the terrarium in bright, indirect light but never direct sun. Just as the interior of a car heats up when the sun shines through the windows, plants in a closed terrarium left in the sun will cook. When watering, it is better to add a little at a time, as it is difficult to remove any excess. Use a turkey baster to control the volume. The soil needs to be moist but not wet.

1

2

3

CREATING A TERRARIUM

1. Start with a dry container so material will not adhere to the walls. Add an inch or two of washed gravel to the bottom. This acts as a moisture reservoir.
2. Place a thin layer of activated charcoal (available in the aquarium section of pet stores) on top of the gravel.
3. Top it off with moistened potting mix, and then add your plants. Depending on the breadth of your container and what you plan to plant, you could make one area deeper, creating the illusion of a rolling landscape.

CONTAINER
RECIPE

1. Red air plant
2. Spanish moss

AIR Plants

These tropical plants are ideal for the beginner container gardener because they require no soil to grow and can thrive despite unintentional neglect.

GROWING AIR PLANTS ▲

Air plants (*Tillandsia* sp.) grow naturally on the trunks of trees, branches, and rocks, so no potting mix is needed for them to thrive. They get all the water and nutrients they need through their leaves, which can be fine-textured or thick and come in shades of green, silver, pink, and red. Spanish moss is a familiar air plant in the coastal South, but there are many others with showy forms. (These are usually sold with houseplants.) Place them in a closed glass container or on an attractive platform underneath a bell jar. You can also mount air plants on cork bark or driftwood. Or create a more modern look by hanging plants in clear glass globes. Air plants like bright, indirect light. Water them about once a week by rinsing the leaves with water and shaking off the excess. That's it!

AN EASY INDOOR PLANT

African violets provide nonstop indoor flowers when given the right growing conditions. That's important. If you have a spot with the right light, moisture, and temperature they like, you can hardly fail.

African violets flourish in bright, indirect light. An east window is ideal because the morning sun is gentle, but the light is reasonably bright all day. African violets like to be warm. Don't keep them too close to a leaky or single-pane window in the winter, because their ideal ambient temperature is 70 degrees Fahrenheit year-round.

Watering is not difficult, but the plants will be so much healthier if you use a little care. Allow tap water to stand overnight so that the fluorine can evaporate and it can become room temperature. Either water from the base by adding water to a saucer, or use care not to wet the leaves when watering from the top. The easiest way to grow African violets is in a self-watering container. Add water and fertilizer in the outer pot, and they will soak through the unglazed inner ceramic pot as needed. Feed with a liquid food for African violets by mixing it with their water according to label directions.

Topiaries

These graphically shaped plants add flair to your home and take up little space indoors.

WHAT TO PLANT

Most topiaries at garden centers are created from English ivy (*Hedera helix*), but myrtle and rosemary are also great options. English ivy topiaries that are pretrained on metal forms, like the lollipop and globe shapes shown at right, add interest to your home without taking up much real estate. English ivy does best near a bright window and can be enjoyed indoors for short periods if you wet (not mist) the leaves each week to keep them from drying out, which will invite spider mites.

Rosemary prefers to live outside but can last the winter indoors. Bright light and good drainage are musts. Allow the plants to dry out slightly between waterings, and don't let them stand in saucers of water. Move them outside as soon as the chance of frost has passed.

For myrtles, good drainage is important and soil should be damp but not stay wet. Myrtles respond well to pruning. Foliage production slows in winter, so most training and shaping occurs when plants are growing in the spring and summer. Be sure to mist plants often; heating systems can dry them out. If myrtle leaves curl or drop, your plant was dry for too long. If so, toss it. Myrtles rarely survive once they've completely dried out.

CARING FOR TOPIARIES

The light requirement for your topiaries will vary based on the plant, but you'll need to water so the soil says moist but well drained. If you find you're watering your topiaries frequently, it may be time to repot. Select the next-size-larger container, use quality potting soil, and gently loosen the bound roots before you replant. In warmer weather, feed your topiaries with a water-soluble fertilizer, such as Miracle-Gro All Purpose Plant Food, twice a month. In cooler weather, feed with a half-strength solution of water-soluble fertilizer every four to six weeks. To keep orbs and other shapes lush and free of bare spots, rotate the pots and trim the plants to encourage equal growth on all sides.

CHOOSE THE RIGHT POT

You can create a harmonious display by planting in a well-proportioned container. Choose a pot that is at least half as tall as the height of the topiary, or go taller for shorties.

SEASONAL
Arrangements

Keep color going year-round in your home with this guide
for accenting your indoor pots with seasonal plants.

VARY YOUR POTS
WITH THE SEASONS

Freshening your indoor containers every
season doesn't have to mean starting from
scratch on a quarterly basis. Instead, you
can use one to three plants as the base of
your container and swap out the others to
add height, color, or visual interest. As your
plants change, you may want to move the
pot to different locations in your home, for
better lighting or to suit your mood for that
season. Here and on pages 138-139, you'll
find seasonal container recipes to help get
you started.

BUILDING YOUR BASE

When deciding on the base plants for the
container, you'll need one for height and
one for trailing to give you a balanced pot
with seasonal flexibility. Here are some
options:

- Button fern
- Rabbit's foot fern
- Autumn fern
- Ornamental hybrid oregano, such as
  'Kent Beauty'
- Variegated creeping fig
- Silver lace fern

SEASONAL PLANTS ▶
FOR SPRING

To freshen the container for the spring
season, try gloxinia, pink kalanchoe,
burgundy oxalis, or primrose.

CONTAINER
RECIPE

1. Fern
2. Rex begonia
3. Kalanchoe
4. Ornamental oregano

SEASONAL PLANTS
FOR SUMMER
To add seasonal interest in the
summer, try angel-wing begonia,
Guzmania bromeliad, zinnia, calla
lily, or anthurium.

CONTAINER
RECIPE

1. Bromeliad
2. Autumn fern
3. Variegated fig vine

For the cooler fall months, you could use Aster Croton, mums in shades from yellow to burgundy, or Rex begonia to create seasonally appropriate containers.

CONTAINER RECIPE

1. Fern
2. Variegated fig vine
3. Mum
4. Rex begonia

SEASONAL PLANTS FOR WINTER

For the winter, try poinsettia, paperwhites, Christmas cactus, amaryllis in shades of white to peach to red, burgundy oxalis, or red or white cyclamen paired with dwarf conifers.

CONTAINER RECIPE

1. Fern
2. Variegated fig vine
3. Cyclamen
4. Asparagus fern (protasparagus myriocladus)

CONTAINER RECIPE

1. Oregano
2. Tomato
3. Sweet basil
4. Cherry tree
5. Pear tree
6. Gloriosa daisy
7. Blueberry
8. Crepe myrtle

Edibles

EDIBLES
Contained

A few pots provide garden-fresh harvests without the space and work a big garden requires, yielding the unrivaled flavor of homegrown produce in smaller, more manageable quantities.

WHY YOU SHOULD GROW EDIBLES IN CONTAINERS

Container-grown fruit, vegetables, and herbs are an excellent way to bring fresh produce to your table. Plus, there are real advantages to growing in pots. If you have been unable to rotate your vegetables to different beds in your garden, growing in containers will give your garden plot a rest. Also, by growing in pots, you'll use less water overall, and you can give plants everything they need to produce, including the perfect soil, water, fertilizer, and light.

PICK THE RIGHT POT, LOCATION, AND TIME OF YEAR

Containers for vegetables need to be a generous size. Put a standard determinate tomato plant in an 18-inch-diameter pot, and it will look like it is swimming in an ocean for about a month; then as it grows and the leaves fill out, it will look just right. The location needs to receive 6 to 8 hours of direct sun, or plants will be weak and unproductive. It's important to pay attention to your zone's frost date for spring and fall. These are the bookends of planting. You'll find seed packages will list when to plant before or after a frost date. Consult a *Farmers' Almanac* or the National Oceanic and Atmospheric Administration website for this information.

START WITH SEEDS OR PLANTS?

You can begin with either plants or seeds. Plants will give you a quicker start, and if you have limited space inside your home to devote to starting plants from seed and storing them before temperatures outside warm up, that's a good idea. However, seeds are much less expensive, and they are simply better for some crops, such as radishes, carrots, okra, and a variety of herbs.

CONTAINER RECIPE

1. Nasturtiums
2. Alfalfa
3. Bok choy
4. Mint
5. Mix of salad greens: bok choy, mesclun, arugula

PICKING THE RIGHT PLANTS ▶

A wide variety of vegetables can be grown in containers, so you can choose based on your family's culinary preferences as well as your space. Choose plant varieties that are bred for use in containers, and read the label to find out if they'll need support to grow. Stick to dwarf varieties when possible. Consider mixing tall plants with medium-size and even trailing ones (for example, trailing rosemary). This will create an interesting focal point.

GROWING FRUIT IN POTS

With new varieties in the marketplace, growing fruit trees and shrubs in containers is becoming easier; however, planting in containers is not for all fruiting plants, so be sure to read the labels. Dwarf blueberries and even full-size ones grown as a screen are fairly low maintenance. Strawberries, especially the everbearing selections, are pretty with flowers, fruit, and foliage. They can grow along the edge and allow something taller to be planted behind them, as long as the pot is large enough and the sun can reach both. Patio peaches, such as 'Bonfire', are manageable in pots, and they offer handsome foliage all season. Kumquats, Meyer lemon, and calamondin trees yield nicely in containers, as long as there is a way to protect them when the weather gets below 50 degrees. Keeping the pots on dollies that can be rolled in and out of the house will help gardeners in cooler zones.

PLANTS TO POTENTIALLY AVOID

Squash, pumpkins, gourds, and melons are vigorous vines that take up a lot of space, probably too much room considering their potential harvest. If you find a variety with "bush" in its name, you can possibly grow it in a container if you really want to. Other space hogs are corn and indeterminate large-fruited tomatoes (unless you are going to use a railing for support).

PLANTING AND WATERING

When planting your edibles, use a quality bagged potting mix, and water your plants regularly. While even moisture is best for all growing plants, be careful not to let them dry out. This can cause problems with blossom end rot and cracking. Sun is another important factor. Having at least 6 hours is a must for fruits and vegetables.

PROVIDE APPROPRIATE SUPPORT ▶

You'll need to create supports for vining vegetables. Indeterminate tomatoes need spacious, sturdy support, like the railing of a porch or deck. Determinate tomatoes can be grown with a tepee made of bamboo or stakes lashed together at the top. Large tomato cages will also work. The small tomato cages are best used for eggplants and peppers. This is an opportunity to be creative, fashioning supports for your plants while making your garden interesting.

HARVESTING

Harvest regularly, and have someone harvest for you if you travel. Once the seeds mature on plants such as beans and cucumbers, the plant will stop producing.

EDIBLE FLOWERS

It's always nice if the edibles you grow are pretty as well as productive. To help with this, consider putting some edible flowers into the mix. Both the foliage and flowers of chervil, chives, cilantro, dill, fennel, rosemary, and thyme are edible. Other edible blossoms you may not have considered include pansies and violas, daylilies, calendula, chicory, nasturtiums, pineapple sage, purslane, and snapdragon, to name a few. After your kale, collards, and broccoli bloom, you can eat those flowers as well. Why eat flowers? Because adding floral color to a salad or as a garnish on a plate makes it all the more appetizing, especially if you are gardening with a child. Just be careful that none of the flowers you pick for your plate have been sprayed with pesticides.

EDIBLE
Inspiration

Fruits, vegetables, and herbs are practical food-producing plants, but they also add ornamental beauty to your garden.

INCORPORATE EDIBLES INTO YOUR FLOWER GARDEN ▼

Containers with edibles don't have to be confined to your deck, patio, or indoors. They can be blended into your existing garden beds to add interest and beauty all year long. For example, blueberry bushes have wonderful fall color that can be a great accent to your existing plants. Evergreen rosemary, with its aromatic thin leaves, can be lovely in containers in your garden beds along a sidewalk, driveway, or entryway; passersby can enjoy the touch and smell of the fragrant stems.

EDIBLE GROUPINGS

For ease, group the pots of edibles that have similar watering needs. Most edibles in pots will need a regular amount of water, but some plants will need daily watering to stay healthy. Grouping these pots together makes it easier to tend to them over time.

TASTE THE DIFFERENCE

With many citrus varieties, you'll be amazed at the difference between them. It's worth trying them out to taste the difference between some of the common varieties found in stores. Lemon varieties like 'Improved Meyer Lemon' are a great choice for containers.

GROWING CITRUS

To enjoy beautiful citrus plants, gardeners in most areas need to plan on a winter getaway spot for their citrus pots. Citrus can enjoy many months outside but will need a place in a bright indoor window (preferably facing south) for the winter months. If you live in an area that never dips below 50 degrees, your citrus plants should be fine outside year-round. Some varieties of mandarin orange are cold resistant to the teens.

PICKING THE RIGHT VARIETIES

Citrus plant varieties that are 15 inches or less in height are perfect for containers, and you'll find that garden centers have really increased the varieties available for purchase. Even before seeing the fruit, you'll be able to enjoy the plant's dark, glossy green leaves and fragrant flowers. Good options to consider include:

- LEMON: 'Ponderosa', 'Improved Meyer Lemon', 'Variegated Pink Eureka'
- LIME: 'Kieffer'
- MANDARIN: 'Dancy', 'Encore', 'Satsuma', 'Tangelo' mandarin hybrid
- KUMQUAT: 'Meiwa', 'Nagami'

GROWING TIPS FOR CITRUS

- CONTAINER: Plant in a medium to large pot (10 to 20 inches) with good drainage.
- WATERING: Water regularly. The plants may need daily watering in hot temperatures.
- FERTILIZE: Fertilize with a slow-release fertilizer because of the need for constant watering. Look for fertilizers specifically for citrus.
- TEMPERATURE: Bring containers indoors when temperatures drop below 50 degrees, and keep inside until the temperature warms back up. Once inside, keep watering (not as much) and regularly mist the foliage. Avoid placing the plants near heating vents as they will dry out the plant.

Citrus

You don't have to live in Florida or on the West Coast to grow citrus. Dwarf varieties are well suited to growing in containers, allowing gardeners everywhere to enjoy the beauty and flavor of these plants.

Approach

There are endless possibilities for planting in warm and cool seasons. Look for season-appropriate plants in garden centers, and use our guide below for perfect combinations that will produce throughout a season.

COOL-SEASON CONTAINERS

Look to cool-season edibles to add color to the garden. Colors can range from rich greens to dark purples. If the plants don't live through the winter, replant them again in early spring before the last frost for another round of fresh taste and colorful display.

KALE: Planting kale and other leafy greens gives a variety of texture and color to your cool season pots. From the bumpy, slender leaves of 'Lacinto' to the kinky curly edges of 'Dwarf Blue Curled Vates', there is so much variety with kale. Look for interesting textured leaves, color, and a variety of heights to bring interest to your pot garden. Also try cabbage, broccoli, or mustard greens.

LETTUCE: Potted lettuce won't provide endless salads, but it's ideal to supplement store-bought greens and to use for sandwiches. Varieties come in bright green to dark purple.

CILANTRO: Also known as 'Coriander', cilantro is a popular herb for Asian and Mexican dishes. It's a fast grower, so harvest one-third of the plant at a time to get the most out of it. Other alternatives include parsley, chives, or dill. In some areas, herbs will come back for another burst of growth before the last frost date.

WARM-SEASON CONTAINERS

TOMATOES: Plant tomatoes in large pots or urns, and choose varieties bred for containers, such as 'Patio' or 'Sweet 'n' Neat', which can be grown without support. You can also plant a determinate ('Better Bush', 'Bush Early Girl', 'Bush Goliath') or dwarf indeterminate ('Husky Cherry Red') that can be supported using a tomato cage or homemade tepee. If you have an area next to a railing or fence that gets adequate sunlight, you'll have more planting options because the vines can use it for support.

ZUCCHINI: One plant can be quite prolific in an 18- to 24-inch pot. Also consider growing crookneck, straightneck, or pattypan squash.

CHIVES: Perennial herbs such as chives or thyme can remain in a small pot year-round. Other good options are creeping thyme or 'Spicy Globe' basil.

Berries

Containers are a wonderful option for growing berries, particularly if you have limited space or don't want berries overtaking your backyard. With water and sunshine, you'll be on the road to a bountiful harvest.

STRAWBERRIES

Strawberries are versatile and simple to grow in containers. They like the sun, so place your containers in an appropriate spot. They also like moist, well-drained soil with lots of organic matter. To keep them healthy, feed them monthly with a liquid blossom-booster fertilizer.

Plant strawberries in March or April after the last frost. Start by buying certified disease-free plants that are labeled as such from the garden center. For a reliable harvest, choose at least two different selections of the June-bearing type that produce one crop a year in the late spring or early summer, depending on your climate. Multicrop, everbearing types don't perform as well in the South. Plant disease-resistant 'Allstar', 'Apollo', 'Earliglow', and 'Surecrop' in the Upper through Lower South (USDA Zones 6–8). For the Coastal and Tropical South (USDA Zones 9–10), go with tasty 'Rosa Linda', 'Strawberry Festival', and 'Sweet Charlie'.

GROWING TIPS FOR STRAWBERRIES

When preparing your containers, fill them with quality potting soil—not topsoil or "garden soil." Three plants are plenty for a pot, window box, or hanging basket. You'll need to replace the plants in your containers every three years. If you have a problem with birds robbing you of ripening fruit, run a string between two poles at the ends of your container and attach strips of aluminum foil to it. The flashes of reflected light will spook the birds.

A SWEET REWARD

Strawberries are one of the most rewarding and fun fruits to grow. With plenty of sun, well-drained soil, and a monthly fertilizer, you can sit back and reap the rewards! Have a little fun growing them in a kitchen garden with a large colander or any container that allows for adequate drainage.

◄ BLUEBERRIES

These beautiful berries with their white to pinkish small flowers in the spring are easily grown in containers because of their shallow-growing root system and your ability to adjust the soil's acidity. They also need a full-sun location. Because they are *not* self-pollinators, you'll need to plant at least two different varieties so they can cross-pollinate; this will result in larger berries and bigger yields. Look for 'Southern Highbush' or 'Rabbiteye' varieties to produce best in Southern zones. Those suited for containers include 'Sunshine Blue', 'Top Hat', and 'Misty'.

GROWING TIPS FOR BLUEBERRIES

- CONTAINER: The size of the pot matters. If you start with a 20- to 24-inch pot, within two seasons the plant most likely will need to move to a large barrel-style container. You may want to start with the larger container to allow room for growth without having to repot.
- SOIL: Blueberries thrive in acidic soil that is loose and well drained, so be sure to adjust the potting mix. Look for an acid soil mix for camellias and azaleas. Adding small amounts of peat moss and perlite will enhance your potting mix.
- WATERING: Make sure the pots stay moist or regularly watered. To make this easier, consider irrigation for pots.
- FERTILIZE: Avoid fertilizing the first year, and then lightly fertilize one time in the spring the following year. Thereafter use a slow-release acid-forming fertilizer to keep your plants healthy.

▲ BLACKBERRIES

Choose the thornless and dwarf varieties for your container garden. Even the dwarf varieties may need staking to help support the plant and for easier management. Blackberries need full sun, rich soil, and good drainage. Dwarf varieties to look for are 'Baby Cakes', 'Black Satin', 'Triple Crown', and 'Thornfree'. Look for fruit starting in midsummer, and plan to pick berries daily.

GROWING TIPS FOR BLACKBERRIES

- CONTAINER: Avoid planting in pots that have previously grown potatoes, tomatoes, or eggplant as they can transfer any disease they may have had to blackberry plants.
- SOIL: Blackberries like neutral soil, so you can use regular high-quality potting soil.
- WATERING: Water plants regularly, but avoid oversoaking them.
- FERTILIZE: Fertilize in early spring with a slow-release fertilizer.
- PRUNING: Blackberries are biennial canes, which means they produce fruit the second year. To maintain the plant and ensure a continued supply of berries, cut only the canes (the plant stems) that have already bloomed and fruited, so you're not removing next season's crop.

HARVESTING BROCCOLI

It's best to harvest broccoli before the buds begin to swell or turn yellow. After cutting the main head, there will be additional shoots that will provide more blooms. Broccoli tends to be better grown in the fall.

Broccoli

This vibrant green vegetable is an easy— and often unexpected— option for container gardening.

BROCCOLI BASICS

Broccoli, one of the easiest crops to grow in the cabbage family, is a handsome plant with big gray-green leaves. Although you can grow it from seed, broccoli transplants are available at most garden centers, and they give you a healthy head start.

Many areas of the country have two seasons of growth, with one in early spring and another in fall. For Southern gardeners, you're not likely to get the large broccoli heads seen in grocery stores due to the shorter cool season. Varieties for fall planting include 'Di Ciccio', 'Green Comet', and 'Waltham 29'. For spring, look for 'Lieutenant' and 'Artwork Stir-Fry,' varieties that can tolerate warmer temps. Place containers in a sunny spot. Watch the top of the stem for the developing flower buds—that's the broccoli—appearing 2 to 3 months after planting. When harvesting, cut the stem 5 to 6 inches below the head. Once you cut the main head of broccoli, smaller side shoots will form on the stalk. These are perfect for steaming or stir-frying.

GROWING TIPS FOR BROCCOLI

- CONTAINER: Choose a pot that is at least 18 inches wide to give the broccoli enough room to grow.
- SOIL: Use a high-quality potting mix.
- WATERING: Broccoli needs to be watered regularly to maintain steady growth.
- FERTILIZE: Use a 10-10-10 fertilizer and apply 3 weeks after planting.

Eggplant

This glossy, plump vegetable with its firm, meaty flesh is a delicious container option.

PLANTING EGGPLANT

Like its cousin, the tomato, eggplant is a summer favorite. For container-grown eggplant try 'Little Prince', 'Pot Black', 'Amethyst', 'Patio Baby', 'Fairy Tale', 'Hansel', and 'Gretel'. You can use transplants to get a jump start, but if you want a more unusual variety, you'll likely need to start from seed. Place the pot in a sunny location. It's a good idea to stake the container when you plant to support the plant later when it's heavy with fruit. Using small tomato cages is a great way to stake eggplant. When it's time to harvest, use shears to cut the fruit before it's too large. This will help to avoid bitterness. You'll need to leave 1 to 2 inches of stem on the fruit.

GROWING TIPS FOR EGGPLANT

- CONTAINER: Use a large, 15- to 24-inch pot.
- SOIL: Use a high-quality potting mix.
- WATERING: Eggplant needs regular watering during the growing season.
- FERTILIZER: Feed eggplant with a solution of liquid 10-10-10 fertilizer every month during growing season.

Lettuce

Possibly the easiest edibles to grow are salad greens,
and they grow wonderfully—and look beautiful—in pots. You'll
love the rich colors and textures—not to mention the great flavors.
Curly, wavy, and frilly leaves in bright greens, reds, and browns
complement fall flowers such as violas or pansies.

GETTING STARTED GROWING LETTUCE

The most economical way to grow the greatest range of selections is by starting from seeds for mixed lettuces, mesclun, or a blend of greens. When sowing, dampen the soil and sprinkle the seeds on top of it; cover them with a thin layer of soil. Gently water daily until they germinate. Thin the seedlings as they grow, and use them in salads.

If you're a novice or just want to get started a bit faster, start with plants that are ready to go into the ground or a pot. You can buy lettuce (*Lactuca sativa*) selections individually or as mixes. Don't plant transplants too deeply, and water gently.

PLANTING LETTUCE

Plant your lettuce in a spot that gets 4 to 6 hours of sun daily. Use a lightweight potting mix in your containers, and be sure your pot has a hole in the bottom for good drainage. Consistent soil moisture is important, so water regularly.

HARVESTING LETTUCE

Expect to begin harvesting leaf lettuces 45 days after planting and semi-heading selections in about 50 days. The best way to harvest loose-leaf types is to pick only the outer leaves near the bottom so the plant can keep growing—which will continue until the weather gets too hot or too cold. For romaine or butterhead, cut off the entire head. To store lettuce, soak it immediately in an ice water bath for 5 minutes. Drain well, and store in a plastic zip-top bag in the refrigerator.

CREATE THIS CONTAINER

1. Choose a large, low bowl with drainage holes, and fill it with a good-quality soil-less potting mix. This bowl is 12 inches in diameter.
2. Use transplants for a quick and easy harvest. This bowl contains 3 (4-inch) transplants of colorful and tasty Wildfire mix lettuces. Keep plants evenly moist. Harvest from the outside of the plants so they'll keep growing.

LEAFY
Greens

These plants offer wonderfully unique texture and flavor when cooked, and they look great in the garden when mixed with pansies, mums, and other cool-season plants.

GROWING GREENS

Easy and versatile, leafy greens thrive in the cooler weather of fall and early spring. They cook down a lot, so plant more than you think you'll need. Greens need full sun—at least 4 to 6 hours per day—and rich soil to quickly produce leafy growth. Plant them in a large pot that is at least 14 inches in diameter with good drainage, and be sure to keep the plants evenly moist.

FEEDING GREENS

Choose a fertilizer that's high in nitrogen to promote the growth of leaves, not flowers. Try Dynamite Organic All-Purpose (10-2-8).

HARVESTING GREENS

Harvest the outer leaves from the bottom, moving up, as soon as the leaves are large and the plant is established. Wash the leaves thoroughly before cooking them.

GET TO KNOW SOME GREENS

All of these leafy greens like the same growing conditions.

'JOI CHOI' BOK CHOY: The green leaves with creamy white veins offer a subtle variegated look. A relative of Chinese cabbage, bok choy can be cooked or eaten raw.

'REDBOR' KALE: Ruffled leaves and red stems add texture and color to your containers. Try it in soups and stews.

'RED GIANT' MUSTARD: Green leaves tinged with purple make a striking focal point in a pot. It's a peppery green that can be wilted, added fresh to sandwiches, or mixed into salad greens.

'RHUBARB' SWISS CHARD: As ornamental as it is tasty, the red stems glow in the autumn sun.

Okra

Okra is an edible you can grow to eat, but you will also enjoy it for its height, foliage, and hibiscus-like bloom.

GROWING OKRA

This is a fast and easy vegetable to get started from seed. Sow seeds (tip: soak seeds in water overnight) when temperatures reach the mid-70s. They need the heat to grow. When seedlings reach 2 inches in height, thin them so they're 6 to 12 inches apart. Try dwarf varieties like 'Annie Oakley II', 'Baby Bubba', or 'Cajun Delight'; regular varieties can get top heavy in pots. Place the pots in full sun. Okra plants take about two months to start flowering, and pods form immediately after the flowers fade.

At the peak of the season in the summer, you'll need to cut pods every 2 to 4 days (even daily, if you have a prolific plant) to prevent them from getting too big and tough. Use clippers or scissors to minimize damage to the plant. Store the pods in the refrigerator, collecting from several days if need be until you have enough to prepare for a meal.

GROWING TIPS FOR OKRA

- **CONTAINER:** If using seeds, you'll want to use as wide a pot as possible—at least 20 inches would be best for each plant. There could be up to 3 to 4 plants in a container.
- **SOIL:** Okra likes neutral soil.
- **WATERING:** Water the plants regularly, keeping the soil well drained.
- **FERTILIZE:** Okra will produce fruit without fertilizer, but if you want to give your plants an extra boost, fertilize after the first pods set with a 10-10-10 fertilizer.

CONTAINER-FRIENDLY OKRA VARIETIES

'HILL COUNTRY HEIRLOOM RED': Drought-tolerant plant bears 6-inch-long green pods with reddish ribs and tips. Pods are great for pickling. Texas heirloom.

'GOLD COAST': Sweet, mild, spineless, light green pods up to 6 inches long. Well-branched plants tolerate heat and drought.

'COW HORN': Large, curved pods up to 14 inches long are best picked at 5 to 6 inches. Thomas Jefferson enjoyed this heirloom in his Monticello garden.

There are a wide array of
chile peppers of all hues
and heat levels. Another
perk: most are relatively
easy to grow in containers.

PLANTING PEPPERS

Peppers offer beautiful foliage and delicious fruit, and they come in many sizes, shapes, and Scoville units—the measurement of how hot they are. Depending on the variety, peppers need 70 to 90 days from the time transplants are potted until they're ready to be picked. If you start from seed, the growing time will obviously be a bit longer.

The plants usually grow to 18 to 24 inches during the summer. Those plants with small peppers can stand unassisted, but any of the large pepper plants need to be staked or grown in a tomato cage to prevent them from falling over. It's best to put those supports in place when you first plant. Some ideal container varieties include 'Mini Bell' in red and yellow, 'Cajun Belle', 'Golden Cayenne', 'Poblano-Ancho', 'Shishito Sweet'. There are so many varieties, you may want to choose a variety based on the type of heat you want to grow.

When harvesting peppers, it's best to use clippers to remove them to avoid breaking a branch. You can pick peppers at any time; they're never too small or too young. But, as they grow, they often change color, improving in flavor. So, if you're growing sweet bell peppers, pick the green ones, but leave some on the plant to turn yellow, orange, or red.

GROWING TIPS FOR PEPPERS

- CONTAINER: Each pepper plant needs to be planted in its own container that's at least 18 inches in diameter.
- SOIL: Use a high-quality potting mix.
- WATERING: During flowering and fruiting season, peppers need regular watering to keep the soil moist.
- FERTILIZER: Fertilize as the plant is becoming established and before the flowering. Once it's set with flowers, too much fertilizer will bring more foliage than fruit.

Peppers

Peppers offer a range of flavor from delightfully sweet to fiery heat. Their variations in color make for beautiful, functional containers.

Potatoes

From dense, waxy varieties to fluffy, starchy versions, potatoes are a crowd-pleaser and a tasty option for a container garden.

PLANTING POTATOES

To plant potatoes, you need potatoes, but not the ones from the grocery store since those are treated with growth inhibitor. Instead, purchase seed potatoes that are carefully raised to be disease free. If the seed potato is large, cut it into 1¼-inch pieces that each contain an eye (the bud that causes an indentation in the surface). Let the cut pieces air-dry for a few days before planting them. Plant the potatoes pieces in early spring, two weeks before the last frost date, or in the fall.

Potatoes are easily grown in large containers—look to the whiskey barrel–size to house one plant. Set the seed piece on top of 6 inches of soil, and then cover with 2 inches of soil. Over time, as the tops grow, gradually add more soil until the pot is filled. There are many container-appropriate varieties to choose from, including 'Cranberry Red', 'Irish Cobbler', 'Sebago', and 'Yukon Gold'.

Harvesting potatoes is a bit like digging for treasure. Potatoes are ready about 2 to 3 months after planting. Dig for them when the plant begins to bloom.

GROWING TIPS FOR POTATOES

- **CONTAINER:** You'll need a large container, at least 40 inches in diameter.
- **SOIL:** Use a high-quality potting mix.
- **WATERING:** Potatoes require regular watering until the leaves turn from yellow to brown and then die down.
- **FERTILIZER:** Potatoes are heavy feeders, so prepare to use a potato-specific fertilizer or a tomato fertilizer to keep them healthy.

CHECK THE FROST DATE

Frost kills tomato plants, so you don't want to leave plants outside or plant them before checking your area's frost-free date.

Tomatoes

Tomatoes are the epitome of summer. Growing your own allows you to try hundreds of varieties and enjoy the incomparable flavor of homegrown.

DETERMINATE VS. INDETERMINATE

Tomatoes are either "determinate" or "indeterminate." Determinate types are busy and will set their fruit and ripen over several weeks. Standard tomato cages available at any garden center will generally provide enough support. Indeterminate types are vinelike and will continue to grow and produce over a period of months. This type needs more support.

AVOID PLANTS THAT ALREADY HAVE FLOWERS OR FRUIT

Don't buy these plants. You want plants that will invest all their energy during the first weeks after planting into building strong roots, stems, and leaves to support the plant throughout its life, not flowering or ripening fruit. Your patience on the front end will yield more tomatoes later. If your plants already have fruit and flowers, you can pinch them off before planting.

WATERING TOMATOES

Keep tomato plants consistently moist to prevent the skins of the fruit from cracking. If you're not sure if you need to water, stick your finger in the soil. If the top inch of the soil feels dry, it's time to give your tomato plants a drink.

GREAT CONTAINER TOMATOES

Tomatoes suited to containers include 'Bush Early Girl', 'Bush Goliath', 'Husky Cherry Red', 'Litt'l Bites', 'New Big Dwarf', 'Patio F Hybrid', 'Sunset Falls', 'Super Bush', 'Tiny Tim', 'Totem', 'Tumbling Tom', and more. Stagger your plantings so you can have a season full of tomatoes.

CHERRY
Tomatoes

Don't overlook these tiny tomatoes in favor of larger varieties. What they lack in size they make up for in flavor and number—you'll be harvesting these tasty bites by the bucketful.

PLANTING CHERRY TOMATOES

You can choose from hundreds of selections for your containers—your local nursery should have a good selection of plants and seeds and you'll find more online. The plants will produce clusters of round, oblong, or pear-shaped fruit in varying sizes, colors, textures, and flavors. Choose a pot that's at least 5 gallons (18 inches in diameter) with adequate drainage. Fill it with a good-quality potting mix that contains water-retaining polymers. Tomatoes need to be planted deep to establish a strong stem and roots while still having plenty of room for their roots to expand. If you're planting transplants, pinch off the lower leaves of the plant halfway up the stem before planting them. Then, bury each plant up to its first two leaflets. Firm the soil around the stem, and then mulch to help conserve moisture. Cherry tomatoes like a lot of sun, too, at least 6 hours of full sun.

PICKING THE RIGHT PLANTS

If you don't have a lot of room, 'Micro-Tom' and 'Florida Basket' are ideal for pots and need no staking. Try these other varieties, too:

'CHOCOLATE CHERRY': Full of flavor with acidic, dark red fruit on a strong plant

'SWEET BABY GIRL': The perfect tiny tomato produces sweet, tasty red fruit on a bountiful, compact plant

'YELLOW GRAPE': Mild, sweet flavor, its clusters of fruit ripen to a bright yellow

'SUPERSWEET 100': The name says it all—one of the sweetest and most prolific to grow, it is a vigorous vine

'SUN GOLD': Very sweet, abundant, and ripens to a bright orange on a robust plant

FRONT-YARD HERBS

If it's not sunny enough in your backyard, put your herbs out front. An urn ringed with mondo grass becomes a formal perch for these practical plants.

CONTAINER
Herbs

Herbs are agreeable to almost any type of container and have few requirements. They get along beautifully in a variety of combinations because most have compatible light and water needs.

KEEPING HERBS HAPPY

Herbs don't tolerate soggy roots, so you'll need to plant them in containers such as ceramic pots that provide controlled drainage. If the container you use doesn't have a way for water to escape, add one large drainage hole or several small ones around the bottom. Herbs like a minimum of 5 hours of direct sunlight every day and need to stay well watered (and well drained). If grown in small pots, herbs dry out quickly, so start with containers that are at least 10 to 15 inches in diameter.

HERB MAINTENANCE

Trim your herbs often to keep them from flowering. When they bloom, their flavor diminishes, and the growth of tasty new foliage slows.

GROWING CONTAINER HERBS

Remember, many herbs flourish quickly, and some, such as rosemary, get very large.

1. Start with a good-sized pot, at least 10 to 15 inches in diameter.
2. Fill it with a good-quality potting soil, and plant several herbs together.
3. Leave an inch of space between the top of the soil and the rim of the pot for a "water well."
4. If the herbs become too crowded after a few months, dig one or two out of the pot, and plant them in their own container, leaving the empty space for the remaining plants to fill in.

SELECTING HERBS TO GROW

Which herbs do you select? In addition to being tasty, herbs such as basil (see page 180), parsley, dill, chives, cilantro, rosemary, sage, oregano, and thyme provide great color and texture to a mixed container.

FOUR EASY HERBS

CHIVES: All parts of this herb are edible. An established plant sends up new leaves in early spring and blooms before summer's onset. After flowering, cut the plant back. You'll need to water regularly for new growth.

PARSLEY: Flat-leaf parsley has the best flavor for cooking. The curly type's slightly bitter taste makes it an excellent garnish; you can also use it as a decorative addition to containers. Pair it with pansies for a pretty companion.

CILANTRO: This musky-flavored herb resembles parsley but has a much more assertive flavor. (If you tend to get them confused, plant them in separate containers.) Use it copiously in the spring because it will succumb to the heat, and it doesn't dry or freeze well. Plant again in the cool season for a longer growing period. It makes a beautiful combination with pansies.

ROSEMARY: One of the most fragrant herbs, rosemary is great for beginners. Selections vary in height from 1 to 6 feet, so choose a smaller variety for your containers. Prostrate or creeping selections rarely grow taller than 1 to 2 feet with short, narrow leaves. They make excellent potted plants and topiaries. In the Upper and Middle South, you'll need to bring your containers inside when a hard freeze threatens.

Basil

Basil is the king of herbs—it adds fragrance to any garden and is so versatile in the kitchen. Plus, it thrives in the South with little care, so it's a great option for new gardeners.

SELECTING THE RIGHT VARIETY

'Genovese' is the classic basil grown for pesto. Plant other selections for a variety of flavors that can be used in different ways in the kitchen. Try the compact 'Italian Cameo' or 'Spicy Globe' basil, or plant 'Mrs. Burns' Lemon' or 'Lime' to enjoy citrus flavors that work well with fish. Use the purple leaves of 'Round Midnight' and 'Purple Ruffles' to flavor vinegars. A large leaf of 'Mammoth Sweet' basil can cover a tomato sandwich. Spicy 'Cuban' basil will pump up your salsas. Order online from johnnyseeds.com or cooksgarden.com.

GROWING BASIL

Basil is an easygoing annual herb. It needs warmth and likes 4 to 6 hours of sun a day. Plant it in a spot that gets morning light as well as protection from late-afternoon sun. It prefers slightly moist, well-drained soil that has been amended with organic matter. Set out transplants or sow seeds in containers. Add mulch such as pine straw or finely shredded pine bark to help keep the roots cool.

HOW TO KEEP BASIL HAPPY

Don't overwater it. Feed your basil using an organic product, such as Maxicrop Liquid Seaweed & Fish or other seaweed-based fertilizer (3-1-1, planetnatural.com). Gather it regularly to encourage new leaves and help delay flowering, because once it starts blooming, the leaves will toughen and lose flavor.

TRY A NEW BASIL VARIETY

'CUBAN': Small leaves grow on a globe-shaped plant. Ideal for containers, it adds a spicy kick to salsas.

'PURPLE RUFFLES': Frilly, purple leaves and intense fragrance combine in the most beautiful basil in the garden.

'MAMMOTH SWEET': Here's the pick for lots of pesto. Large, crinkled, light green leaves can even be used whole on sandwiches.

'GENOVESE': This is the favorite basil for pesto. You can also use it fresh in recipes or as a garnish. It's sometimes called sweet basil.

'RED RUBIN': Use it fresh in recipes, as a garnish, or for colorful vinegars. Also known as 'Opal', it is very fragrant.

'SWEET THAI': Licorice-scented leaves bring out the flavors of other ingredients. Use it in Asian dishes, such as stir-fries.

FIND YOUR
Zone

Southern Living divides the South into five broad climate zones: Upper South (US), Middle South (MS), Lower South (LS), Coastal South (CS), and Tropical South (TS), which correspond to those of the United States Department of Agriculture (USDA) Plant Hardiness Zone Map. The Upper South is in USDA Zone 6, the Middle South in Zone 7, the Lower South in Zone 8, the Coastal South in Zone 9, and the Tropical South in Zone 10. For those living outside the Southeast, check the USDA's plant hardiness zone map to find what zone you are.

It's important to note that because the USDA map reflects minimum yearly temperatures, it functions solely as a cold-hardiness map. In the South, however, heat is as much a limiting factor as cold. Therefore, when we give a plant a *Southern Living* climate zone rating, we take into account both summer heat and winter cold. For example, if we recommend astilbe as a permanent plant for your area, we mean that it will not only survive your winters but also endure your summers—and that it will perform satisfactorily for you. We won't recommend astilbe for the Coastal or Tropical South because, although it takes winters there, in summer it melts faster than ice sculptures on a cruise ship.

UPPER SOUTH (US)

USDA ZONE 6

This region experiences the longest winters and shortest summers in the South, but summers are still hot and sticky. Fortunately, sizzling Southern temperatures rarely last long. Plants that need cool nights and long periods of winter chill do well here. Cold winters bring constraints, however. Frozen soil means that dahlias, cannas, gladiolus, and other summer-flowering bulbs must be dug up in fall and stored over the winter. Crepe myrtle, camellias, and figs may not be cold-hardy in all areas. The last frost occurs anytime from mid-April to the first 10 days of May.

MIDDLE SOUTH (MS)

USDA ZONE 7

This region forms a transition zone between warm-weather and cool-weather growing zones. Here, you often encounter plants from the Northeast, the Midwest, and the Northwest growing alongside Southern natives. Summers are hot and, in most places, humid. The last spring frost generally occurs in the last two weeks of April.

LOWER SOUTH (LS)

USDA ZONE 8

Spring comes early to the Lower South. Daffodils, flowering quince, and winter daphne open their buds in February. Though summer droughts are common, torrential downpours more than make up the difference. Snow is rare, but ice storms are not. The last frost generally occurs in the first two weeks of April.

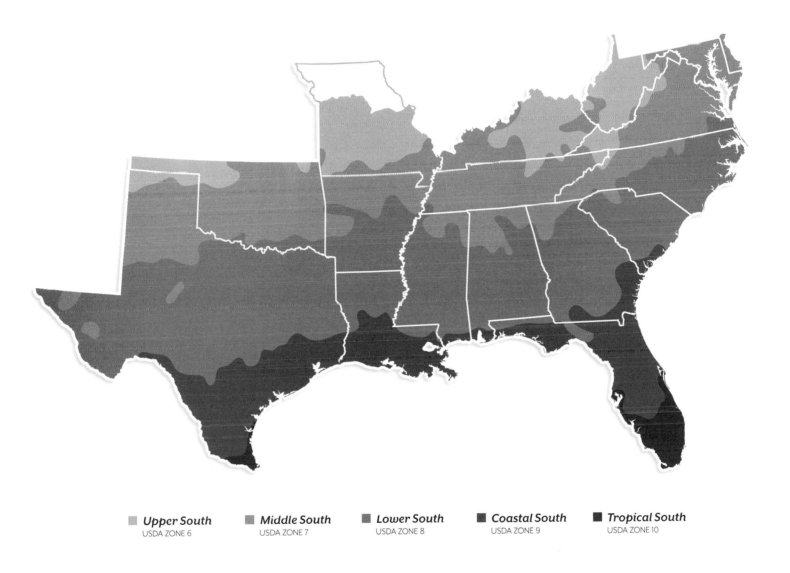

Upper South	**Middle South**	**Lower South**	**Coastal South**	**Tropical South**
USDA ZONE 6	USDA ZONE 7	USDA ZONE 8	USDA ZONE 9	USDA ZONE 10

COASTAL SOUTH (CS)

USDA ZONE 9

Two large bodies of water—the Atlantic Ocean and the Gulf of Mexico—rule the Coastal South. Their close proximity ensures that winters are mild and brief but summers are long and humid. The last spring frost usually comes in the second or third week in March. Spring commences in January, when the oriental magnolias and common camellias bloom.

TROPICAL SOUTH (TS)

USDA ZONE 10

Truly its own gardening world, the Tropical South rarely feels frost. In fact, the lowest temperature on record for Miami is 30 degrees. Whereas most of the South deals with dry summers and wet winters, a large portion of the Tropical South reverses that pattern. All sorts of lush, exotic plants with strikingly colorful blooms and foliage flourish here. To outsiders, this region can seem like a paradise. But the lack of winter chill comes at a price. Apples, azaleas, forsythia, hostas, hydrangeas, and many other temperate plants fail here.

Credits

PHOTOGRAPHY CREDITS

Getty Images:
page 19, table: Westend61; page 171: Johner Images; istock/Getty Images Plus: page 23, Bravo chrysanthemum: hakkousei; page 26, *F. japonica*: y-studio; page 30: ClarkandCompany; page 49, fertilizer: arto_canon; page 100, pedestal arrangement: onepony; page 153, tomatoes and peppers: Geo-grafika; page 165, bok choy: winning7799; page 165, mustard greens: JTBOB888; page 165, Swiss chard: Tony Baggett; Hemera/Getty Images Plus: page 45, impatiens: Nancy Tripp; Photo/Alto Agency RF Collections: page 26, Boston ivy: PhotoAlto/Isabelle Rozenbaum; Iconica: page 126: ML Harris; Photographer's Choice RF: page 165, kale: Paul Thompson; Photolibrary: page 167, okra growing: Joshua McCullough; E+: page 152: Funwithfood; page 153, zucchini: tacojim; Maskot: page 179, rosemary: Hakan Jansson

iStock: page 170: Mypurgatoryyears

page 144, 169: Jennifer Causey (prop styling: Graham Yelton); page 158: Cedric Angeles

WITH SPECIAL THANKS TO:
Mindy and Ray Estep, Terry and Ken Hooks, and Joyce and David Melton

Index

paperwhite narcissus, 89, 139
papyrus, 20
parsley, 152, 178, 179
patio peaches, such as 'Bonfire', 145
peace lily (*Spathiphyllum* sp.),
    44, 110, 119
pear tree, 140
peat moss, 15, 18, 19, 43, 128, 157
pennisetum, 20, 25
    'Fireworks', 56
    'Sky Rocket', 98
pentas, 80, 98
peperomia, 131
peppers, 146, 168–169
    container for, 169
    fertilizing and watering, 169
    harvesting, 169
    supports for, 169
    transplants, 169
    varieties of, 'Mini Bell' in red and
        yellow, 'Cajun Belle', 'Golden
        Cayenne', 'Poblano-Ancho',
        'Shishito Sweet', 169
perennials, 31, 42, 44, 45, 51, 56, 65,
    77, 106
periwinkle, 78
'Perle von Nurnberg' echeveria, 84
perlite, 15, 19, 128, 157
Persian shield (*Strobilanthes
    dyerianus*), 29
pesticides, on edible blossoms, 147
petunia, 25, 31, 40, 48, 60, 62, 98
    'Easy Wave Pink', 56
    'Supertunia Sangria Charm', 57
    'Supertunia Vista Bubblegum', 57
    'Surfinia White Improved', 76
philodendron, 44
    'Prince of Orange', 98
phlox, 'David' summer, 77
pineapple sage, edible blossoms, 147
pinecones, 12, 48
pink arrowhead vine, 103
'Pink Beauty' caladium, 28
placement of pots, 32–35, 36, 72
    cluster, for big impact, 37
    distinct front and back, 33
plantable bags, 15
plant for quick impact, 40–41
    step-by-step, 41
planting, 50, 51, 52, 56, 58, 72–73, 80.
    See also design.
    basics, 30–31
poinsettia, 110, 139
polka dot plant (*Hypoestes* sp.), 45
polymers, in potting mix, 18, 47
polystyrene, 19
ponytail palm, 115
porch, 45, 52, 57, 62–65, 94

portulaca, 98
portulacaria, 'Red Stem', 84
Possumhaw branches, 91
potatoes, 157, 170–171
    container for, 170
    container varieties of, 'Cranberry
        Red', 'Irish Cobbler', 'Sebago', and
        'Yukon Gold', 170
    fertilizing, 170
    seed potatoes, 170
    watering, 170
pothos (*Epipremnum aureum*),
    98, 103, 119
pothos, 'Neon', 103
pot lifter, 42
pots, 9, 10–17
    drainage hole, 12, 13
    fixing cracks in containers, 17
    foot, 12, 13
    Protecting Your Pots, 51
    types of, 14–17
        cast stone, 10, 16
        concrete, 10, 16
        fiberglass, 15
        glazed ceramic, 15
        hypertufa, 15
        lightweight foam, 15
        plantable bags, 15
        resin, 10, 16
        terra-cotta, 10, 15, 16, 17, 35, 97
        wire with a coir liner, 16, 97, 98, 99
    unsticking terra-cotta, 16
potting bench, 42–43
potting mix, 9, 10, 12, 15, 17, 18–19, 20,
    30, 33, 34, 41, 42, 43, 46, 47, 49, 51, 80
    for blackberries, 157
    for blueberries, 157
    for broccoli, 159
    for cherry tomatoes, 174
    and drainage, 13
    for edibles, 146
    for eggplant, 160
    in hanging baskets, 99
    for herbs, 177
    for indoor plants, 112, 125, 126
    ingredients in, 19
    keeping the mix fluffy, 18, 19
    labeled for orchids, 128
    for living wall frame, 102
    make your own, for succulents, 85
    for peppers, 169
    for planting bulbs, 89
    for potatoes, 170
    reusing, 18
    sinking, 19
    storing, 42
    for strawberries, 154
    for succulents, 85, 86

weeds in, 48
for window boxes, 79
primrose, 136
'Prince of Orange' philodendron, 98
privacy, screening for, 70, 71, 79. *See
    also* screening for privacy.
pruning, 20, 48, 73
    blackberries, 157
    indoor plants. 126
    myrtle topiaries, 134
    plants on a tuteur, 106
'Pseudobracteatum' Chinese
    evergreen, 120
pteris ferns, 131
pumpkins, 145
Purple Heart, 23
'Purple Ruffles' basil, 181
purslane, edible blossoms, 147

Q
quince, 90

R
'Rabbiteye' blueberries, 157
rabbit's foot fern (*Davallia fejeensis*),
    119, 136
radishes, 143
'Redbor' kale, 165
'Red Giant' mustard, 165
red hot poker, 25
'Red Rubin' basil, 181
'Red Stem' portulacaria, 84
repetition, 38–39, 62
    of color, 38, 39, 64, 95
    of materials, 64
    of plant forms, 62, 95
    of pots, 62, 70
    of textures, 95
repurposed objects, as containers, 61
resin pots, 10, 16
reusing plants, 50
reusing potting mix, 18
Rex begonia, 51, 130, 136, 138
'Rhubarb' Swiss chard, 165
Rieger begonia, 45
romaine, 163
rooftop garden, 82, 105
roots, 10, 12, 18, 46, 51, 71, 80, 102, 128
    of blueberries, 157
    of cherry tomatoes, 174
    of established plants, 34
    and fertilizer, 49
    grown through the drainage hole, 13
    oxygen for, when watering, 46
    and repotting plants, 19
    of succulents, 85
    and wilting plants, 47
'Rosa Linda' strawberries, 154